Cambridge Elements ≡

Elements in Religion and Monotheism
edited by
Paul K. Moser
Loyola University Chicago
Chad Meister
Bethel University

NECESSARY EXISTENCE AND MONOTHEISM

An Avicennian Account of the Islamic Conception of Divine Unity

Mohammad Saleh Zarepour

The University of Manchester

CAMBRIDGE
UNIVERSITY PRESS

CAMBRIDGE
UNIVERSITY PRESS

University Printing House, Cambridge CB2 8BS, United Kingdom

One Liberty Plaza, 20th Floor, New York, NY 10006, USA

477 Williamstown Road, Port Melbourne, VIC 3207, Australia

314–321, 3rd Floor, Plot 3, Splendor Forum, Jasola District Centre, New Delhi – 110025, India

103 Penang Road, #05–06/07, Visioncrest Commercial, Singapore 238467

Cambridge University Press is part of the University of Cambridge.

It furthers the University's mission by disseminating knowledge in the pursuit of education, learning, and research at the highest international levels of excellence.

www.cambridge.org
Information on this title: www.cambridge.org/9781108940054
DOI: 10.1017/9781108938112

© Mohammad Saleh Zarepour 2022

First published 2022

A catalogue record for this publication is available from the British Library.

ISBN 978-1-108-94005-4 Paperback
ISSN 2631-3014 (online)
ISSN 2631-3006 (print)

Necessary Existence and Monotheism

An Avicennian Account of the Islamic Conception of Divine Unity

Elements in Religion and Monotheism

DOI: 10.1017/9781108938112
First published online: May 2022

Mohammad Saleh Zarepour

The University of Manchester

Author for correspondence: mohammadsaleh.zarepour@manchester.ac.uk

Abstract: Avicenna believes that God must be understood in the first place as the Necessary Existent (*wāǧib al-wuǧūd*). In his various works, he provides different versions of an ingenious argument for the existence of the Necessary Existent – the so-called Proof of the Sincere (*burhān al-ṣiddīqīn*) – and argues that all the properties that are usually attributed to God can be extracted merely from God's having necessary existence. Considering the centrality of *tawḥīd* to Islam, the first thing Avicenna tries to extract from God's necessary existence is God's oneness. The aim of the present Element is to provide a detailed discussion of Avicenna's arguments for the existence and unity of God. Through this project, the author hopes to clarify how, for Avicenna, the Islamic concept of monotheism is intertwined with the concept of necessary existence.

Keywords: Avicenna, monotheism, Necessary Existent theology, Proof of the Sincere

ISBNs: 9781108940054 (PB), 9781108938112 (OC)
ISSNs: 2631-3014 (online), 2631-3006 (print)

Contents

1 The Avicennian Conception of Islamic Monotheism

The cornerstone of Islamic faith, regardless of its interpretation by different branches of Islam, is *tawḥīd*: there exists one and only one God Who is the ultimate ground of everything in the universe. 'There is no god but God' – or, as it is expressed in the Quran (37: 35 and 47: 19), *lā ilāh illa Allāh* – is the most fundamental claim that every Muslim must testify to and endorse (*šahāda*).[1] The message of divine unity is also conveyed in other Quranic verses with slightly different wording: the phrases '*mā min ilāh illa Allāh*' (3: 62 and 38: 65) and '*lā ilāh illa Huwa*' (2: 163, 2: 255, etc.), for example, are repeated respectively two and twenty-six times in the Quran, meaning, again respectively, 'there is no god but God' and 'there is no god but He'. The repetition of this notion is a sign of the unique and crucial role it plays in the web of Islamic beliefs. It should therefore come as no surprise that, from the Quranic perspective, denying the unity of God (*širk*) or ascribing to Him a partner (*šarīk*) is the only sin that God never forgives:

> Truly God forgives not that any partner be ascribed unto Him, but He forgives what is less than that for whomsoever He will, for whosoever ascribes partners unto God has surely fabricated a tremendous sin. (4: 48)

Thus understood, *tawḥīd* is the Islamic expression of monotheism; accordingly, *širk* – the opposite of *tawḥīd* – can be construed as the expression of polytheism. The verse just quoted therefore highlights that the fundamental message of Islam is the denial of polytheism and the endorsement of monotheism. Indeed, conjoining this observation with the content of other verses, it can be argued that, from the point of view of the Quran, to be a truly religious person in general is precisely to accept the uniqueness of God.

The Quran states that '*'inna al-dīn 'ind Allah al-islām*' (3: 19). If we interpret '*islām*' as referring exclusively to the religion of the followers of the prophet Muhammad, then the whole phrase must be understood as emphasising that, in the sight of God, the true religion is Islam and the followers of other religions (including Judaism and Christianity) cannot be considered truly religious people. Such an interpretation is implausible, however, because at least one significant figure – the prophet Abraham – lived before the time of the prophet Muhammad and yet the Quran describes him as a true believer in *islām* – that is, a *muslim* (3: 67). This shows that in the context of the Quran, *islām* and *muslim*

---

[1] In references to the Quran, 'x: y' refers to verse y of chapter x. Unless otherwise mentioned, all translations of Quranic verses – including the verses mentioned in the quoted passages whose other parts are translated by myself – are borrowed from Nasr (2015). On the notion of *šahāda* in Sunni and Shia Islam, see Ahmed (2016, pp. 137–9).

must have a broader meaning than the terms *Islam* and *Muslim* as they are understood within the sociocultural categorisation of religions.[2] Indeed, the literal meaning of *islām*, which seems to fit better into the Quranic context, is submission (to God). On this construal, a *muslim* is a person who has truly submitted to God and His commands; such wholehearted submission is plausible only if there is no god but He.[3] Indeed, the first and the most obvious precondition of true and full submission to God seems to be to concede His unity. That is why the Quran's description of Abraham as one who submits to God is complemented by an emphasis that he was not a polytheist:

> Abraham was neither a Jew nor a Christian, but rather was an upright (person), one who truly submits, and he was not one of the polytheists. (3: 67)[4]

We may conclude that, according to the Quran, the true religion is *islām* in the sense of sincere submission to God and a truly religious person is a *muslim* in the sense that she/he endorses God's unity and sincerely submits her/ himself to God. Thus, being a *muslim* in its Quranic sense has no simple connection to being a bearer of the sociocultural label 'Muslim'. Some people might describe themselves as followers of the prophet yet have not truly submitted to God: since they do not truly accept the core of monotheism and do not believe that all power, knowledge, and goodness are entirely God's, they would not be *muslim* in the Quranic sense even if they are labelled 'Muslims'. On the other hand, there might be people whom a sociocultural mapping would classify as followers of other religions (e.g., Jews and Christians), but who are true *muslims* in the Quranic sense. In the sight of God, the true religion is *islām* and the core tenet of *islām* is the sincere endorsement of monotheism and full submission to God:

> God bears witness that *there is no god but He*, as do the angels and the possessors of knowledge, upholding justice. *There is no god but He*, the Mighty, the Wise. (3: 18)

> *Truly the religion in the sight of God is submission.* Those who were given the Book differed not until after knowledge had come to them, out of envy among themselves. And whosoever disbelieves in God's signs, truly God is swift in reckoning. (3: 19)[5]

Given the centrality of monotheism in Quranic theology, it is by no means surprising that, in the intellectual history of Islam, the first two goals in any

---

[2] For a discussion of different senses of *islām* and for references to recent works on this issue, see Ahmed (2016, chap. 1).
[3] See Cole (2019) and Donner (2019) for studies which support this understanding of the meaning of *islām* in the Quran.
[4] My translation. [5] Emphases are mine.

theological discussion have been to establish the *existence* and the *oneness* of God. Naturally, how these targets are approached hinges on how God is understood. Among the early Muslim theologians and philosophers there was no consensus on this question, and consequently there was no unique strategy for defending the monotheistic essence of Islam. For example, for the first Muslim philosopher, al-Kindī (d. 870), the two targets merge because, inspired by Plotinus, he understands God as the True One (*al-wāḥid al-ḥaqq*). So, for al-Kindī, the existence of God is tantamount to God's true oneness. To prove the existence of God, al-Kindī puts forward an argument based on a combination of a priori claims and factual observations, trying to show that the plurality we see in the world cannot be caused except by the True One.[6] By contrast, being more faithful to Aristotelian doctrine, al-Fārārbī (d. 950) understands God as the First Existent Who is the cause of all other things while It is Itself uncaused. So al-Fārārbī first shows – by appeal to a more or less Aristotelian argument based on the impossibility of infinite regresses – that there is such an existent, and then argues that the First Existent can have no duplicate.[7] From Avicenna (d. 1037) onwards, however, things change.

Avicenna believes that God must be understood in the first place as the Necessary Existent (*wāǧib al-wuǧūd*). In his various works, he provides different versions of an ingenious argument for the existence of the Necessary Existent – the so-called Proof of the Sincere (*burhān al-ṣiddīqīn*) – and argues that all the properties that are usually attributed to God can be extracted merely from God's having necessary existence.[8] In other words, being-a-necessary-existent is the most fundamental attribute of God which entails all His other attributes. Considering the centrality of *tawḥīd* to Islam, the first thing Avicenna tries to extract from God's necessary existence is God's oneness. However, to achieve this goal, at least in some of his works, he first establishes the *simplicity* of the Necessary Existent. So, in at least some places, he apparently sees divine simplicity as a bridge between divine necessity and divine unity. This does not mean that Avicenna has in practice abandoned the priority of *tawḥīd* over all other divine attributes: indeed, *tawḥīd* can be rendered as a general doctrine about divine unity which includes not only the uniqueness of God among all beings but also the internal

---

[6] For al-Kindī's account of the existence and unity of God, see the third section of his *On First Philosophy* in *The Philosophical Works of al-Kindī* (2012, pp. 26–41). For secondary studies on this issue, see Marmura and Rist (1963) and Adamson (2007, chap. 3).

[7] See Menn (2011).

[8] I have borrowed the phrase 'the Proof of the Sincere' as the translation of '*burhān al-ṣiddīqīn*' from Legenhausen (2005). Two alternative translations, used by Adamson (2016, p. 126) and Rizvi (2019, sec. 3.3), are respectively 'the Demonstration of the Truthful' and 'the Proof of the Veracious'. See Legenhausen (2005, p. 44, n. 1) on the exact meaning of the term *ṣiddīqīn*.

simplicity of God.[9] These two components of *tawḥīd* represent, respectively, the extrinsic and the intrinsic unity of God.[10] The doctrine of *tawḥīd* can accordingly be understood as stating that (1) there are not multiple gods and (2) there is no multiplicity in the nature of God. So as long as Avicenna proves (1) and (2) before moving on to the other attributes of God, he is faithful to the idea of the priority of *tawḥīd* over the other divine attributes, regardless of whether (1) is proved by appealing to (2) or vice versa.

Avicenna's approach later became so prevalent that there are barely any post-Avicennian Muslim philosophers or theologians who demur from describing God as the Necessary Existent or from the possibility of extracting God's other attributes from God's having necessary existence.[11] All the disagreements concern either the details of the Proof of the Sincere or the details of the arguments for establishing some of God's attributes based on God's having necessary existence.[12] This indicates that for many centuries the philosophical theology of Islam has been centred on the Avicennian understanding of God. Of course this does not prevent post-Avicennian thinkers like al-Ġazālī (d. 1111) from criticising other aspects of Avicenna's conception of God (aspects beyond God's being the Necessary Existent) and considering Avicenna's image of God incompatible with the image of God in the Quran.[13]

The aim of the present Element is to provide a detailed account of Avicenna's arguments for the existence and unity of God. Understanding the Avicennian notion of *efficient causation* in the same manner that contemporary analytic metaphysicians understand the notion of *ontological dependence*, I offer and defend revised versions of the Avicennian arguments for the existence of a unique necessary existent in which the existence of every other thing is grounded. But before engaging with the subtleties of Avicenna's arguments and presenting my own reconstruction of them, it is worth mentioning a few general points about Avicenna's methodology. In particular, I should highlight the striking similarities between Avicenna's approach and Anselm's perfect being theology, with which analytic philosophers of religion are more familiar.

---

[9] This of course does not include necessary existence, which, from Avicenna's point of view, is the characteristic attribute of God.

[10] Wisnovsky (2003, p. 148).

[11] On the reception of the notion of the Necessary Existent by post-Avicennian Muslim philosophers, see Benevich (2020).

[12] On the reception of the Proof of the Sincere by post-Avicennian philosophers, theologians, and mystics, see Davidson (1987, chaps. IX and X), Legenhausen (2005), and Morvarid (2008, 2021).

[13] See, among others, Marmura (1964) and Burrell (1993).

2 Avicennian Necessary Existent Theology versus Anselmian Perfect Being Theology

There are two different understandings of how the different attributes of God are related to each other. According to the first, which we may refer to as the *single-divine-attribute* (SDA) doctrine, there is a unique divine attribute which entails, either directly or indirectly, all the other divine attributes. On this approach, all the attributes of God are somehow dependent on a certain fundamental attribute of Him and can accordingly be extracted from it. As a result, God can be fully described by that specific attribute. Thus, if we prove the existence of something which possesses that specific attribute, we have established the existence of God. Richard Swinburne seems to be endorsing SDA when he writes: 'almightiness entails *all* the divine properties; and thus, since it is the nature of an almighty being to be almighty, an almighty being is characterised by these properties necessarily'.[14]

By contrast, according to the *multiple-divine-attributes* (MDA) doctrine, there is more than one fundamental divine attribute. These attributes cannot be reduced to each other either directly or indirectly, and God's having each of them must be investigated independently from the others. On this approach there is no unique attribute through which we can fully describe God.[15]

For analytic philosophers of religion, the most famous defender of SDA in the history of theology and philosophy is Saint Anselm of Canterbury (d. 1109).[16] For Anselm, there is one fundamental divine property – that is, being-that-than-which-no-greater-can-be-thought – from which all other divine attributes can be derived. To consider some examples, for Anselmian theists, being omnipotent, omniscient, and omnibenevolent can be easily concluded from being absolutely perfect. Therefore, if we can prove the existence of an absolutely perfect being (or, more precisely, the existence of the being than which no greater can be thought), we have established the existence of an omnipotent, omniscient, and omnibenevolent being.[17]

However, Anslem is not the first philosopher to have developed a theological system based on SDA: Avicenna followed a similar approach. Although Anselm and Avicenna disagree on what the most fundamental attribute of

---

[14] Swinburne (1988, p. 229), my emphasis.

[15] The phrase 'single-divine-attribute doctrine' is taken from Schlesinger (1988). The distinction between SDA and MDA is discussed by Hestevold (1993). The MDA approach is held by, among others, Wierenga (1989).

[16] Anselm was born around four years before Avicenna's death and died two years before al-Ġazālī.

[17] For defences of the Anselmian SDA doctrine, see, among others, Morris (1987), Schlesinger (1988), Franklin (1993), Rogers (2000), Nagasawa (2017), and Speaks (2018). For criticisms of this doctrine from different perspectives see, among others, Mackie (1982, chap. 3, sec. b), Hestevold (1993), Oppy (1995, chaps. 1 and 8), Sobel (2004, sec. II.4), and Diller (2019).

God is, they both endorse SDA. For Avicenna, the most fundamental divine attribute is necessary existence. Neither Avicenna nor Anslem believes that God has a definition in the Aristotelian sense, but they share the view that God can be identified through a unique fundamental attribute.[18] In the same manner as Anslem sought to prove all God's attributes from God's being-that-than-which-no-greater-can-be-thought, Avicenna maintained that all God's attributes can be drawn out from God's being-the-necessary-existent and put forward many ingenious arguments to establish that attributes like simplicity, unity, immateriality, atemporality, and unchangeability can be deduced solely from necessary existence.[19] For Avicenna, God's absolute perfection is entailed by His necessary existence. For Anslem, it is the other way around: God's necessary existence is entailed by His absolute perfection.

There is another notable commonality between Avicenna and Anslem: both try to establish the existence of God by presenting entirely a priori arguments aimed at proving the existence of a being which has the fundamental attribute they ascribe to God. Although there is no consensus among Avicenna scholars on whether his Proof of the Sincere is an ontological argument in the sense that Anslem's argument is, it seems indisputable that both of these arguments are free from a posteriori features. These strong methodological connections between the two philosophers thus tempt us to develop a modern systematic Necessary Existent theology which can be considered as the Islamic–Avicennian counterpart of the modern Christian–Anselmian perfect being theologies. The later sections respond to this temptation in a preliminary fashion by providing reconstructed versions of Avicenna's arguments for the existence and unity of the Necessary Existent.

It must be emphasised that my primary concern in the following discussion is the philosophical strength of the arguments I offer, rather than historical accuracy and textual fidelity. So although the kernels of all arguments are extracted from Avicenna's texts, I do not hesitate to compromise on certain details (even concerning claims to which Avicenna is proudly committed) where this might make my arguments more coherent and compelling for a contemporary reader. Were I asked to label my project, I would describe it as an instance of *analytical Avicennianism*. Inspired by John Haldane, who coined the term 'analytical Thomism' in the early 1990s, the term 'analytical Avicennianism' can be understood as

---

[18] On the indefinability of God for Avicenna and Anslem, see, respectively, Kamal (2016, p. 197) and Logan (2009, p. 91).

[19] On how Avicenna tries to show that the Quranic attributes of God can be deduced from God's having necessary existence, see Adamson (2013, 2016, chap. 18).

referring to the general idea of bridging between Avicenna's philosophy and contemporary analytic philosophy.

3 Basic Notions of the Proof of the Sincere

3.1 Is the Existence of God Self-Evident?

In the first chapter of the first book of *The Metaphysics of* The Healing, Avicenna argues that the existence of God is not self-evident and needs to be established through metaphysics rather than by any other science:

> The existence of God – exalted be His greatness – cannot be admitted as the subject matter of this science (i.e., metaphysics); rather, it is [something] sought in it. This is because, if this were not the case, then [God's existence] would have to be either admitted in this science but searched for in another, or else admitted in this science but not searched for in another. Both alternatives are false. For it cannot be sought in another science, since the other sciences are either moral, political, natural, mathematical, or logical. None of the philosophical sciences lies outside this division. There is [absolutely] nothing in them wherein the proof of God – exalted be His greatness – is investigated. [Indeed,] this is impossible . . . [God's existence] would then have to be either self-evident (*bayyin bi-nafsih*) or [else] something one despairs of proving through theoretical reflection. But it is neither self-evident nor something one despairs of demonstrating; for [in fact] there is a proof for it. Moreover, how can an existence which one despairs of demonstrating be legitimately admitted? It thus remains that the investigation [of God's existence belongs] only in this science.[20]

In this passage, Avicenna considers four different possibilities regarding the existence of God: (1) The existence of God must be proved in metaphysics. (2) The existence of God must be proved in sciences other than metaphysics. (3) The existence of God is self-evident and consequently needs no proof. (4) The existence of God is unprovable. He then rejects the three latter possibilities and concludes that the existence of God must be proved in metaphysics. It is interesting that he insists that the existence of God is neither self-evident nor can be admitted without any proof: this reveals that he does not consider belief in God a properly basic belief in the sense that contemporary reformed epistemologists like Alvin Plantinga do.[21] Since Avicenna rejects the idea that the existence of God can be accepted without any argumentative justification, a fortiori he would disagree with fideists who render religious faith completely

---

[20] Avicenna (2005, chap. I.1, sec. 11). All translations from *The Metaphysics* are by Marmura. The phrases within parentheses and square brackets are, respectively, mine and Marmura's.

[21] On the view that belief in God is properly basic, see Plantinga (1981, 1983). See also McNabb (2019) for the general elements of the reformed epistemology of religious beliefs.

independent of theoretical reason.[22] The existence of God, Avicenna believes, can and must be proved by theoretical reason. He seems, then, to be a proud defender of an evidentialist theism according to which belief in God is justified because there is convincing rational evidence for it. Such evidence – in the absence of which belief in God would be implausible – cannot be provided in any science other than metaphysics, or so Avicenna says in the passage just quoted.

3.2 Proof through Reflection on Existence in Itself

In the last section of the fourth Class of his *Remarks and Admonitions*, Avicenna states that the firmest and noblest way to prove the existence of God is through reflection upon existence qua existence (i.e., existence in itself):

> Reflect on how our proof of the [existence] of the First, His unity, and His freeness from [accidental] attributes (*al-ṣifāt*) does not require reflection on anything other than existence in itself (*nafs al-wuǧūd*). It does not require consideration of His creation and His action, even if such a consideration provides evidence for [the existence of] Him. This method [i.e., reflection on existence in itself] is firmer and nobler [than reflection on God's creation and action]. This is because our consideration of the state of existence bears witness to the existence of Him inasmuch as He is existence; and then He bears witness to [the existence of] other things which are after [or dependent on] Him in existence. Something like this is referred to in the Divine Book: 'We shall show them Our signs upon the horizons and within themselves till it becomes clear to them that it is the truth.' I say that this is a rule for a group of people. It [i.e., the Divine Book] then says: 'Does it not suffice that thy Lord is Witness over all things?' (41: 53). I say that this is a rule for the sincere people (*al-ṣiddīqīn*) who bear witness [to other things] from Him, rather than to Him [from other things].[23]

Here Avicenna distinguishes two different ways of arguing for the existence of God. The first is to reflect on God's creation and actions as a means to argue for His existence; the second is to reflect on existence itself to establish the existence of God. Avicenna believes that the latter approach is more solid and is the one followed by those who are sincere. Thus the Proof of the Sincere aims at establishing the existence of God – together with His unity and His transcendence from accidental attributes – through theoretical consideration of existence in itself.

The first premise of (most versions of) the Proof of the Sincere is therefore that *something exists*. As Avicenna puts it at the beginning of the version of this proof in the metaphysics part of his *The Salvation*, 'there is no doubt that there is

---

[22] Tertullian, Pascal, Kant, Kierkegaard, James, and Wittgenstein are the most famous historical advocates of fideism. In more recent literature, various fideist approaches to the epistemology of religion are defended by, among others, Cupitt (1984), Evans (1998), and Bishop (2007).

[23] Avicenna (1957, vol. 3, chap. IV.29, pp. 54–5), my translation.

existence'.[24] Post-Avicennian philosophers routinely quote this sentence in their reflections upon the Proof of the Sincere,[25] and one might think that it expresses an a posteriori fact, albeit 'with an extremely thin empirical content'.[26] However, it can be convincingly argued that for Avicenna, the sentences 'there exists something' and 'there is existence' express facts that are entirely a priori: this is because these claims can be inferred from the proposition expressed by the sentence 'I exist', and the a priority of the latter is guaranteed by Avicenna's Flying Man Argument.[27] This thought experiment shows that even if a person consists solely of an immaterial (or bodyless) soul who has no contact with the physical world, she/he can still know that she/he exists. In other terms, the Flying Man Argument shows that even if we have no experience of or access to the physical world, we can still entertain our self-consciousness. So, from the perspective of every human being, 'I exist' can be known independently from any experience of the physical world: equivalently, such knowledge can be grasped a priori.[28] Finally, since the argument from 'I exist' to 'there exists something' or 'there is existence' appears deductively valid, and presumably the a priori status of the premise is transferred across the valid entailment, the two latter propositions would be a priori as well.[29]

In the next steps of the Proof of the Sincere, the different states of an existent are taken into consideration. To proceed, we must first look at a couple of distinctions which play crucial roles in Avicenna's proof.

3.3 The Distinction between Essence and Existence

One of Avicenna's main achievements is to establish the distinction between essence (*māhīya*, *ḏāt*, *ḥaqīqa*, and sometimes *ṭabīʿa*) and existence (*wuǧūd*). The essence of a thing is *what* that thing is. The whatness of a thing is independent from whether that thing exists. For instance, that a triangle is

---

[24] Avicenna (1985, p. 566). Avicenna presented the Proof of the Sincere in different places in his *oeuvre*, including but not limited to the metaphysics parts of the following works: (1) *The Salvation* (1985, pp. 566–8) and (2) *Remarks and Admonitions* (1957, vol. 3, chaps. 9–15, pp. 19–27). There is no consensus on where Avicenna proves the existence of the Necessary Existent in *The Metaphysics of* The Healing. See De Haan (2016) in this regard.

[25] Mayer (2001, p. 23).   [26] Morvarid (2021).

[27] For the exact structure and implications of the Flying Man Argument, see, among others, Marmura (1986), Alwishah (2013), Adamson and Benevich (2018), and Kaukua (2020).

[28] It is worth noting that a priority is not the same notion as *innateness*. A proposition is innate if it is given at birth, but it is a priori if it can be known independently from all the experiences we might have of the extra-mental physical world. So there can in principle be non-innate propositions which can be known a priori after birth, as we grow up. For instance, Kant believes that mathematical propositions are non-innate but a priori. For a discussion of Avicennian non-innate a priori propositions and of the claim that 'I exist' is one such proposition, see Zarepour (2020c).

[29] The same line of argument has been put forward by Shihadeh (2008, p. 213, n. 57).

a three-sided geometrical figure or that a human is a rational animal do not depend on whether such things actually exist. Thus, generally speaking, essences of things are distinct and independent from their existences.

Although the distinction between essence and existence has a background in ancient Greek philosophy, it is likely that Avicenna's presentation of this distinction was mainly influenced by the distinction between thing (*šay'*) and existent (or, more generally, between thingness and existence) proposed by the early Muslim theologians (*mutikallimūn*).[30] The thing–existence distinction comes up in the theologians' discussions of certain Quranic verses regarding the nature of God and His creative power. On one hand, there are verses which cast doubt on the idea that God can be considered a thing, even though from the viewpoint of the Quran there is no doubt that God exists. For instance, the Quran says (42: 11) that 'no thing is [even] like a likeness of Him' (*laysa ka-miṯlihi šay'*) and warns (4: 36) people not to embrace polytheism by associating *things* with God: 'And worship God and do not associate any thing with him' (*wa-'budū Allāh wa la-tušrikū bihi šay'ā*).[31] Some early Muslim theologians interpreted these verses as clarifying that God's existence does not imply His being a thing. More generally, it follows from these verses that thingness is not implied by existence, or so those theologians argued.

On the other hand, some verses describe the creative act of God as His addressing non-existent things and commanding them to come into existence. For example, it is stated that 'Our Word unto a thing (*šay'*), when We desire it, is only to say to it "Be!" and it is' (16: 40), and that 'His Command when He desires a thing (*šay'*) is only to say to it "Be!" and it is' (36: 82). These verses can in principle be understood as witnessing that thingness does not imply existence either. There can be things that do not exist yet can still be addressed and referred to. Some early Muslim theologians indeed interpreted these verses in this manner. Coupling these two groups of verses, some theologians concluded that *thingness* and *existence* are completely independent notions. Neither implies the other.

It has been argued that Avicenna's distinction between essence and existence is a rehabilitation of the early Muslim theologians' distinction between thingness and existence.[32] Put otherwise, essence is the Avicennian counterpart for the theologians' thingness. Although the details of this comparison are beyond

---

[30] For the Greek background of the essence–existence distinction, see Cresswell (1971) and Corrigan (1996).

[31] See also 3: 64, 6: 151, 12: 38, 22: 26, and 60: 12. The translations of 42: 11 and 4: 36 are, respectively, Wisnovsky's (2003, p. 147) and mine.

[32] See, among others, Jolivet (1984) and Wisnovsky (2003, chap. 7). On Avicenna's own notion of *thingness* (*šay'īya*) and its commonalities and differences with respect to his notion of *essence*, see Wisnovsky (2000).

the scope of this Element, for our current purposes it is sufficient to have an overall grasp of what the essence–existence distinction means. Such a grasp can be provided by the following passage from *The Metaphysics of* The Healing:

> [T]o everything there is a reality (*ḥaqīqa*) by virtue of which it is what it is. Thus, the triangle has a reality in that it is a triangle, and whiteness has reality in that it is whiteness . . . It is evident that each thing has a reality proper to it – namely, its quiddity (*māhīya*). It is known that the reality proper to each thing is something other than the existence that corresponds to what is affirmed.[33]

The essence (or reality or quiddity) of a thing determines what it is. But the essence of a thing does not determine whether it exists. This is true at least about everything other than God. For instance, it is part of the essence of a triangle that it is a three-sided geometrical shape. A triangle is a three-sided geometrical shape inasmuch as it is a triangle. As a result, triangularity cannot be separated from three-sidedness either in mind or in extra-mental reality. By contrast, existence is not part of the essence of the triangle. Triangularity on its own is neutral with respect to existence. That is why we need to prove the existence of triangles. A triangle inasmuch as it is a triangle does not necessarily exist. Nor is it necessarily deprived of existence. What a triangle is, is independent from whether it exists:

> [W]hen you conceptualise the notion of triangle and relate it to shape-ness and relate it to existence, you find shape-ness intrinsic to the notion of triangle, so that it is impossible to understand that triangle is triangle unless [you know] beforehand that it is necessarily a shape. Similarly, it is not possible to conceptualise the notion of triangle without first conceptualising that it is a shape. But it is not necessary to conceptualise that it is existent. In your conceptualisation of the quiddity of triangle, you do not need to conceptualise that it exists in the same manner that you need to conceptualise that it is a shape. The shape belongs to the triangle and is intrinsic to its subsistence (*qiwām*) inasmuch as it is triangle. It [i.e., triangle] is subsisted by it [i.e., shape] externally, in the mind, and in whatever state it is. But existence is something by which the quiddity of triangle is not subsisted. That is why it is possible that you understand the notion of triangle while you are doubtful about its existence, until it is demonstrated to you, in the first diagram of Euclid's book, that it [i.e., the triangle] is an existent or [at least] a possible existent.[34]

Here Avicenna seems to argue that since our knowledge of what a thing is does not hinge on our knowledge of whether that thing exists, the essence of

---

[33] Avicenna (2005, chap. I.5, secs. 9–10).

[34] Avicenna (1959, chap. II.1, p. 61, ll.4–12); my translation. The last sentence refers to the first book of Euclid's *Elements* in which the triangle is the first geometrical shape whose construction is discussed. See Euclid (1908, vol. 1, p. 241) and Avicenna (1977, p. 20).

things is, at least intensionally, distinct from their existence.[35] More precisely, he says that we can form a concept of things without having any idea of whether they exist. This means that the whatness of a thing does not depend on its existence. For example, although the whatness of a triangle depends on its being a geometrical shape and its being three-sided, it is independent from its existence. That is why to form the concept TRIANGLE, we need to know that it is a three-sided geometrical shape, though we do not need to know that it exists or even that it *can* exist. The essences of things are neutral with respect to existence, albeit God could be an exception to this general rule. To see why, we need to address another distinction which goes hand in hand with the essence–existence distinction: the distinction between necessary and possible existents.

3.4 Different Modalities of Existence

Avicenna's account of the modes of existence plays a crucial role in his investigation of the existence and unity of God; this is not at all surprising given that he understands God as the *Necessary* Existent. Avicenna believes that the concepts of modalities – for example, being necessary, possible, and impossible – are basic and primary concepts which cannot be analysed and reduced to more evident concepts.[36] Any attempt at defining these concepts will at best end in circularity:

> All that has been said of the [things] that have reached you from the ancients in defining this (group of notions) would almost entail circularity. This is because – as you have come across in the [various] parts of the *Logic* – whenever they want to define the possible, they include in the definition either the necessary or the impossible, there being no other way save this. And when they want to define the necessary, they include in the definition either the possible or the impossible. [Similarly,] when they want to define the impossible, they include in its definition either the necessary or the possible.[37]

This of course does not deter Avicenna from proposing certain criteria for identifying these notions and distinguishing them from each other. One of the main goals Avicenna pursues in chapter I.6 of *The Metaphysics of* The Healing is to provide such criteria. Furthermore, in his logical works, Avicenna – like

---

[35] As Wisnovsky (2005, p. 110) has pointed out, Avicenna's discussions of the relationship between essence and existence suffer from underdetermination. Janos (2020) provides a comprehensive account of Avicenna's view on the ontology of essence in itself.

[36] Marmura (1984) provides a detailed commentary on chapter I.5 of *The Metaphysics of* The Healing in which Avicenna introduces the primary concepts of his metaphysics.

[37] Avicenna (2005, chap. I.5, sec. 22).

Aristotle – proposes temporal models of modalities.[38] Nonetheless, these endeavours are by no means aimed at giving non-circular definitions of the modalities: Avicenna persistently denies that such definitions can be found. Interestingly, Avicenna's stance on the primacy and basicness of the modalities has not lost plausibility over the ages: the majority of analytic metaphysicians, especially those who try to explicate such concepts in terms of possible world semantics, concede that the triple of modal notions *possibility*, *impossibility*, and *necessity* cannot be defined in a non-circular manner. While tools like possible world semantics can help us to obtain a more lucid understanding of the modal notions, our comprehension of the nature and exact function of these tools is itself dependent on how the modal notions are understood. For instance, there seems to be no way to understand what a possible world is unless we already know what possibility means.[39]

Bearing in mind that Avicenna has no intention to define modal notions, we may turn to see how he elaborates the different modal statuses that existents may have. Consider an existing object O. Since O exists, it is clear that it was not impossible for it to come into existence. Or, if you wish to avoid the temporal shading of the notion of *coming-into-existence*, we can simply say that it is not impossible for O to exist. This means that the existence of O is either necessary in itself or possible in itself but caused and necessitated through another thing. This is the general logic behind Avicenna's division of existence (and existents) into *necessary in itself* and *possible in itself*:

> The things that enter existence bear a [possible] twofold division in the mind. Among them there will be that which, when considered in itself (*bi-ḏātih*), its existence would be not necessary. It is [moreover] clear that its existence would also not be impossible, since otherwise it would not enter existence. This thing is within the bound of possibility (*imkān*). There will also be among them that which, when considered in itself, its existence would be necessary.[40]

If O is necessary in itself, then its existence is not caused by any other thing. Suppose for *reductio ad absurdum* that O is a necessary existent whose

---

[38] Aristotle's temporal model of modalities can be extracted from passages such as *De Interpretatione*, 9, 19a1–4, 19a32–36, and *De Caelo*, I.11, 281a1–6, and I.12, 281a28–30. Avicenna's temporal model is discussed in, among others, *Syllogism* (*al-Qiyās*) of *The Healing* (1964, chap. I.4) and the *Logic* part of *Remarks and Admonitions* (1957, vol. 1, Method 4). For studies on the Aristotelian and Avicennian versions of these models, see, respectively, Waterlow (1982) and Street (2002, 2013). McGinnis (2011, p. 69) has compellingly argued that, for Avicenna, 'one comes to know time only if one already knows what possibility is'. This means that analysing the notion of *possibility* in terms of temporal notions would not result in a non-circular definition of the former notion. Coupling this observation with the fact that the notions of *impossibility* and *necessity* can be defined in terms of the notion of *possibility*, we can conclude that any plan for providing non-circular definitions of the three main modal concepts (in terms of temporal notions) is doomed to failure.

[39] See, among many others, Blackburn (1984, pp. 213–16).

[40] Avicenna (2005, chap. I.6, sec. 1).

existence is caused by X, which is an existent distinct from O. Since the existence of O is caused by X, O does not exist unless X exists. This is so at least if we adopt the innocent principle that non-existents have no causal power. So O's existence depends on X's. This means that it is not the case that O cannot not exist, since O would have not existed if X did not exist. Hence O's existence is not necessary in itself. But this contradicts the initial assumption. We conclude that if O is a necessary existent, it is not caused by something else. Employing 'the Necessary Existent' as a definite description of God, Avicenna develops the latter line of argument as follows:

> [I]f in His existence the Necessary Existent (*waǧib al-wuǧūd*) were to have a cause, His existence would be by [that cause]. But whatever exists by something [else], if considered in itself, apart from another, existence for it would not be necessary. And every[thing] for which existence is not [found to be] necessary – if [the thing is] considered in itself, apart from another – is not a necessary existent in itself. It is thus evident that if what is in itself a necessary existent were to have a cause, it would not be in itself a necessary existent. Thus, it becomes clear that the Necessary Existent has no cause.[41]

The existence of a necessary existent is not caused by anything other than itself. Nor can anything prevent it existing. On the contrary, if the non-existence of something is independent from everything else, then that thing is *impossible in itself*. Put differently, if nothing can cause something to exist and nothing can prevent its non-existence, then that thing in itself is such that its existence is impossible. Now suppose that O is neither necessary nor impossible in itself. In other words, O is merely possible in itself. This means that the existence and non-existence of O are on a par and neither of them, on its own, preponderates over the other. Therefore, there must be another thing which either causes or prevents O's existence. There must be something that upsets the balance between the existence and non-existence of O and makes one overcome the other:

> [W]hatever is possible in existence when considered in itself, its existence and non-existence are both due to a cause. [That is] is because, if it comes into existence, then existence, as distinct from non-existence, would have occurred to it. [Similarly,] if it ceases to exist, then non-existence, as distinct from existence, would have occurred to it. Hence in each of the two cases, what occurs to the thing must either occur through another or not.

---

[41] Avicenna (2005, chap. I.6, sec. 3). '*Waǧib al-wuǧūd*' means 'Necessary Existence' rather than 'Necessary Existent'. But for Avicenna these two notions are not distinct. The Necessary Existence is the Necessary Existent. So, to avoid further complexities, I follow the common tradition and use the latter translation unless linguistic and/or argumentative constraints require otherwise.

> If [it occurs] through another, then [this] other is the cause. And if it did not exist through another, (then that other is the cause of its non-existence).[42]

It should be borne in mind that the non-existence of O is not always caused by the existence of something else. Rather, it might be the non-existence of something which causes the non-existence of O. Suppose, for example, that O, which is possible in itself, does not exist unless X exists. The non-existence of X can therefore be the cause of the non-existence of O.[43] On the other hand, it seems defensible to assume that the cause of the existence of O is at root the *existence* of something else. The existence of a thing cannot be caused and guaranteed merely by the *non-existence* of something else. This assumption gains plausibility when we note that what Avicenna means by 'cause' in the previous passages is indeed efficient cause, or an agent which bestows existence upon its effect.[44] Moreover, what he has in mind are not merely accidental or auxiliary efficient causes but rather true and essential efficient causes. Not only the origination but also the being of an existing thing at root depends on its true efficient cause. That is why, for example, parents and housebuilders cannot be considered the true efficient causes of, respectively, children and houses. Although parents and housebuilders partially contribute to the origination of children and houses (i.e., to their coming into existence), the continuance of the existence of children and houses, after their coming into existence, does not depend on their parents and builders. This reveals that parents and builders are not the true efficient causes of children and houses, or so Avicenna believes. Now if we understand a cause as something upon which the origination and existence of its effect depend, then it would be obvious that non-existence of a thing cannot be the cause of the existence of another thing. Non-existence is too poor to bestow existence upon anything, let alone to preserve its existence.[45]

Conjoining these three quoted passages we can conclude that existents are exhaustively divided into two categories. Every existent is either necessary in itself (*bi-l-ḏāt*) or necessary through another (*bi-l-ġayr*).[46] Put differently, it is

---

[42] Avicenna (2005, chap. I.6, sec. 4).

[43] Indeed, instead of the phrase that I have added in the parentheses to the end of the previous excerpt from *The Metaphysics of* The Healing, Marmura has added another phrase which accords with the claim that the cause of the non-existence of something is the non-existence of another thing. Since Avicenna's own phrases do not specify whether the non-existence of the thing under discussion is caused by the non-existence or by the existence of another thing, I believe that my neutral addition is more faithful to the main thrust of the passage.

[44] Johnson (1984, p. 162) writes that this kind of causation is what 'the Scholastics called *causa essendi*, cause of existence'.

[45] Richardson (2013) has provided an expanded discussion of Avicenna's treatment of the notion of *efficient cause*. Hereafter, unless otherwise specified, by 'cause' I exclusively mean 'true efficient cause'.

[46] Wisnovsky (2003, chap. 12) elucidates how al-Fārābī anticipates this distinction.

logically evident that the existence of a thing like O is either caused or not caused by something other than itself. If the former is the case, then O is necessary by itself. It does not need anything other than itself to bring it into existence, nor can anything deprive it of existence. On the other hand, if the existence of O is caused by something else, say X, then O cannot not exist as long as X exists. The existence of X necessitates the existence of O. Hence, O's necessity is relative and conditional. It is possible in itself but necessary through another. So there is nothing in the world which lacks both absolute and relative necessity. Every existing thing is necessary, either in itself or through another thing. This idea forms the bedrock of Avicennian necessitarianism.[47]

It is worth emphasising that Avicenna's conception of causation, in the sense delineated here, is totally different from that of contemporary analytic metaphysicians. According to the latter, causation is a (typically counterfactual) explanatory relation between events. For instance, throwing a stone and breaking a window are two events, the first of which can be the cause of the second, or so an analytic metaphysician would say. By contrast, Avicenna understands causation as a relation of existential and ontological dependence between all the existents, no matter what type they are. On this view, X causes Y if and only if Y's existence is bestowed by and dependent on X's existence (or, equivalently, if and only if Y ontologically depends on X). An immediate corollary of this dissimilarity is that, for Avicenna, a cause cannot be temporally prior to its effect. They must exist together simultaneously. This is because, Avicenna tells us, 'the effect needs that which bestows existence on it always, permanently, as long as [the effect] exists'.[48] So although the effect ontologically depends on the cause, the latter does not precede the former in time. That is why fathers and housebuilders cannot be the true efficient causes of, respectively, children and houses, despite the indubitable fact that the former contribute to bringing the latter into existence. Fathers and housebuilders are merely auxiliary and non-essential causes of children and houses:

> It has thus become evident and clear that the essential causes of things through which the existence of the essence of that thing comes about in actuality must exist with it, not having that priority in existence whereby it

---

[47] See also the metaphysics part of *The Salvation* (1985, pp. 548–9) for a clear discussion of the idea that whatever is not necessary (either in itself or through another) does not exist. Avicenna's metaphysical system is worth comparing to modern necessitarian accounts such as that developed by Williamson (2013). Unfortunately, engaging with the subtleties of such a comparison would take us too far afield.

[48] Avicenna (2005, chap. VI.1, sec. 17). See also Avicenna (2005, chap. IV.1, sec. 9). As Rashed (2008, p. 173) emphasises, 'emanation does not take place in time, and anteriority and posteriority have to be understood essentially, not temporally'.

would cease to exist once the effect comes into being, and that this [latter priority] is possible in non-essential or non-proximate causes.[49]

In another place, Avicenna underlines the coexistence of cause and effect as follows:

> Hence, with the existence of the cause, the existence of every effect is necessary; and the existence of its cause necessitates the existence of the effect. The two exist together in time, eternity, or whatever but are not together with respect to the attainment (*ḥuṣūl*) of existence.[50]

Thus, although the cause and its effect coexist both temporally and atemporarily, the existence of the cause has an explanatory priority over that of the effect, or so Avicenna seems to mean by the last sentence of this passage. As we will see, the coexistence of cause and effect plays a crucial role in some interpretations of the Proof of the Sincere.

The relation of ontological dependence – in the sense considered here – is labelled 'entity-grounding' or simply 'grounding' by some analytic philosophers. Grounding is usually considered as an explanatory relation between facts (or propositions expressing them). But some philosophers have generalised this concept to refer to the relation of ontological dependence between all entities, no matter what type they are. For instance, Duen-Min Deng writes:

> [Grounding is] a certain kind of ontological dependence relation that holds between more fundamental and less fundamental entities. So, when the existence of an entity is dependent upon the existence of some other entity or entities in the sense that the former *exists in virtue of* the latter, we say that the former is grounded in the latter, and we call the latter 'the ground' of the former. When the ground contains a plurality of entities, we call each of them a 'partial ground', and call all these entities taken together the 'full ground'.[51]

We can use this terminology to redescribe Avicenna's project in a language more congruent with that of analytic metaphysics. Every existent O is either a fundamental or non-fundamental entity. If O is fundamental, then it is not grounded in any other thing. So O is ontologically independent from any other thing and its existence is necessary in itself. But if O is non-fundamental, then it is fully grounded in something else, X, which can be a compound entity each of whose components is a partial ground of O. O is ontologically dependent upon

---

[49] Avicenna (2005, chap. VI.2, sec. 8).

[50] Avicenna (2005, chap. IV.1, sec. 11). See also the metaphysics part of *The Salvation* (1985, p. 549, ll. 10–11).

[51] Deng (2020, p. 418), emphasis in the original. This account of grounding is developed based on earlier works by Schaffer (2009) and Bennett (2017). Hamri (2018) and Bohn (2017, 2018a, 2018b) adopt the same notion of grounding in their investigations of some arguments for the existence of God.

X and the existence of O is necessary through X. Avicenna's Proof of the Sincere therefore aims to establish that there is one and only one fundamental entity in the world. God is the only fundamental thing whose existence is necessary in itself, and all other things are non-fundamental entities which are eventually grounded in and ontologically dependent on Him.

3.5 The Nature of a Necessary Existent

There is a consensus that, according to Avicenna, a necessary existent has no essence (or quiddity) other than its existence. This is because otherwise its essence would be neutral with respect to existence and non-existence, and so there would have to be a cause to preponderate its existence over its non-existence. But this would mean that its existence would have a cause and would not be necessary in itself. This *reductio* proves that a necessary existent has no essence other than its existence.[52]

The latter doctrine – that a necessary existent has no essence other than its existence – can be read in two different ways: (1) A necessary existent has an essence and its essence is nothing but its existence. (2) A necessary existent has no essence at all. Avicenna wavers between these two alternatives.[53] For example, support for both of them can be found in chapters VIII.4–5 of *The Metaphysics of* The Healing.[54] This uncertainty probably stems from Avicenna's concerns regarding the internal consistency and coherence of his metaphysical system. Each of the two alternative accounts is in some respects in line with the overall picture of Avicennian ontology while in other respects it conflicts with it. Each leads to some sort of exceptionalism in certain parts of his metaphysics. As we saw earlier, two of the main pillars of Avicenna's meta-physics are the following: (a) Everything has an essence, and (b) the essence of a thing is neutral with respect to existence and non-existence. Neither of these is on its own preponderated over the other. Now, if (1) is upheld, then (b) is violated; on the other hand, (2) is in tension with (a). To be clearer, if we assume that a necessary existent has no essence, then it would be an exception to the general rule that everything has an essence. So (a) must be modified to say that everything has an essence *unless it is a necessary existent*. On the other hand, if we stick to (a) with all its generality, then a necessary existent, like any other

---

[52] For arguments in the same vein, though in the context of contemporary analytic philosophy of religion, see Hamri (2018, p. 163; 2019, p. 82).

[53] This issue has been addressed by, among others, Macierowski (1988), Rosheger (2002), Acar (2005, pp. 81–3), McGinnis (2010a, pp. 168–72), and Bertolacci (2012, pp. 275–7).

[54] Avicenna seems to defend (1) in passages like (2005, chap. VIII.5, sec. 2). On the other hand, in passages like (2005, chap. VIII.4, secs. 13–14), Avicenna uses phrases ('*ḥaqīqa wāǧib al-wuǧūd*' and '*ḥaqīqa al-wāǧib al-wuǧūd*') which apparently refer to the essence of the Necessary Existent.

thing, has an essence. But we saw that if a necessary existent has an essence, its essence is identical to its existence. Therefore, it is obvious that for such an essence existence is not on a par with non-existence. If the essence of a thing is its existence, it cannot not exist. The association of such an essence with existence is indispensable. So in this case we have no choice but to give up the generality of (b) and to make an exception to it: the essence of a thing is neutral with respect to existence and non-existence, *unless it is a necessary existent.*

To advance the discussion and provide an unambiguous reconstruction of Avicenna's argument for the existence of God, we need to espouse one of the two alternatives regarding the essence of a necessary existent, and it seems to me that (1) is by and large more plausible than (2). Admittedly, if (1) is true, then it is not the case that all essences are neutral with respect to existence and non-existence. We should therefore accept that different essences enjoy different types of relation to existence and non-existence. However, it is not clear why this idea should be found implausible or even surprising. It sounds quite natural and indeed to be expected that the connection of a necessary existent to existence is by no means comparable to the connection of other things to existence. By definition, existence is not separable from a necessary existent either in extra-mental reality or even in the mind. In fact, the main characteristic of a necessary existent is that its association with existence can be suspended neither in the extramental realm nor even in our imagination. Now, it is not clear why it might be problematic to articulate the latter claim as expressing that existence cannot be detached from the *essence* of a necessary existent. Although the very definition of a necessary existent implies that it is different from other things in terms of its connection to existence, this definition on its own does not imply that such an existent is different from other things in terms of having an essence. So, compared to (2), (1) enjoys more prima facie tenability. My view in this regard can better be understood in contrast with McGinnis' view about the nature of the Necessary Existent:

> [O]ne cannot consider the Necessary Existent independent of its existence, whereas the essence of a given thing can be considered independent of that thing's mode of existence. Therefore, in a very real sense the Necessary Existent cannot have an essence.[55]

McGinnis prefers to retain the generality of (b). So, by insisting that all essences are neutral with respect to existence and non-existence, he denies that a necessary existent could have an essence. Contrary to my inclination,

---

[55] Avicenna (2010a, p. 169).

he inclines towards (2). Of course, I do not claim to have presented a full-blown argument in favour of (1): my intention was just to show that, between the two choices, (1) is more intuitive and requires less argumentative support. Nevertheless, an immediate concern might arise: the idea that a necessary existent has an essence implies that it consists of at least two parts – that is, its essence and existence. Now if we understand God as a necessary existent, we need to accept that God has at least two parts; but this conclusion contradicts the traditional doctrine of divine simplicity. I think, however, that this objection can easily be rebutted. As I argued, if a necessary existent has an essence, its essence must be identical to its existence. Thus, even if the essence of a non-necessary thing does impose an ontological burden additional to its existence, it does not do so in the case of a necessary existent. The essence and existence of a necessary existent are not two *distinct* things with independent ontological weights. Accordingly, the assumption that God is a necessary existent whose essence and existence are identical is perfectly compatible with divine simplicity. In what follows, I assume without hesitation that a necessary existent has an essence which is nevertheless identical to its existence. Even if this view is not always and everywhere defended by Avicenna, it is still a philosophically defensible claim which is consistent with the main components of his metaphysics as we have discussed it so far.

Another important issue about which Avicenna is not entirely clear is whether a necessary existent at root has a cause. There is no doubt that a necessary existent has no cause other than itself. But, again, this claim can be construed in two different ways: (1) A necessary existent has a cause and its cause is nothing other than itself; equivalently, a necessary existent is self-caused. (2) A necessary existent has no cause at all. There is textual evidence for both of these positions in Avicenna's works. For example, we saw earlier that he contends that 'the Necessary Existent (i.e., God) has no cause'.[56] On the other hand, there are places in which he adopts the first interpretation. For instance, in his presentation of the Proof of the Sincere in *The Salvation*, he clearly states that if something caused itself, then it would be a necessary existent.[57] Logically speaking, that a self-caused existent is a necessary existent does not entail the reverse claim that a necessary existent is self-caused. We have not yet excluded the possibility that some necessary existents are self-caused and some others uncaused. Nevertheless, if we assume that being caused or uncaused is part of the nature of a necessary existent, then we would expect that all necessary existents share the same status regarding having a cause. So, from the claim that

---

[56] Avicenna (2005, chap. I.6, sec. 3).   [57] Avicenna (1985, p. 568, ll. 4–8).

a self-caused existent is a necessary one, we can conclude that every necessary existent is self-caused.

Once again, to move forward in the discussion we need to choose one of the two alternatives. It is uncontroversial that Avicenna accepts the irreflexivity of causation for possible existents. He believes that there is no existent which is both possible in itself and self-caused. My preference, however, is to espouse the irreflexivity of causation in its general form and to accept that nothing can be self-caused, regardless of whether it is possible or necessary in itself: I thus contend that a necessary existent is uncaused rather than self-caused. The simple reason for this choice is that although cause and effect coexist simultaneously, the former has, by definition, explanatory priority over the latter. But it does not seem to make any sense to say that something can be explanatory *prior to itself*, even if that thing is a necessary existent. It sounds plausible, indeed, to say that irreflexivity is concealed in the very definition of causation. So, in the sequel, I assume that causation is an irreflexive relation and that every necessary existent is uncaused. Accordingly, I try to reinterpret and reconstruct the Avicennian arguments based on this assumption.

My preferred interpretation fits well with the picture in which a necessary existent is the most fundamental element in a chain of entities which bear the relation of grounding (or, equivalently, ontological dependence) to each other. Analytic metaphysicians usually consider grounding as an irreflexive relation.[58] This means that nothing, including fundamental entities, can ground itself. A fundamental entity is therefore groundless rather than grounded in itself. It is ontologically dependent on and grounded in nothing.

If we accept the idea of the irreflexivity of causation, then the phrases 'necessary by (or in or through) itself' and 'necessitated by (or through) itself' are not coreferential. In fact, by contrast with the former, the latter is empty and does not refer to anything at all. The existence of Y is necessitated by the existence of X if and only if X causes Y. So, if something is necessitated by itself, it causes itself. But since causation is irreflexive, nothing can cause itself and, as a consequence, nothing can necessitate the existence of itself. Thus, although there can in principle exist a thing which is necessary on its own – that is, without being necessitated by anything else – there can be nothing which is necessitated by itself. This means that the existence of a necessary existent is necessary without being necessitated. Its nature is such that it is simply necessary on its own.

---

[58] Irreflexivity of grounding is advocated by, among others, Fine (2001, p. 15), Correia (2008, p. 1023), Schaffer (2009, pp. 364 and 376), Rosen (2010, p. 115), Hamri (2019, p. 78), and Deng (2020, p. 419). On the other hand, this view is criticised by Jenkins (2011) and Bliss (2014, 2018), among others.

Another characteristic of the Avicennian notion of *causation* and its counterparts in modern metaphysics is transitivity. If X causes Y and Y causes Z, then X causes Z. Equivalently, if Z ontologically depends on (or is grounded in) Y and Y ontologically depends on (or is grounded in) X, then Z ontologically depends on (or is grounded in) X. As a result, if there is a chain of existents that are successively caused by each other and ends in an existent O, then the transitivity of causation implies that all those existents are at root caused by and dependent on O. The irreflexivity and transitivity of causation play crucial roles in at least some versions of the Proof of the Sincere. It is by appealing to these properties of causation that we can prove that God is an uncaused and independent being upon which every other being ontologically depends. Even if there are intermediate causes between an existent and God, this cannot prevent God from being the ultimate cause of that existent. An immediate question might arise, however: Should the belief that a necessary existent is uncaused be considered as a deviation from the Principle of Sufficient Reason? Does the fact that the existence of a necessary existent is not necessitated by anything (including itself) entail that its existence is a brute metaphysical fact?

3.6 The Principle of Sufficient Reason

Roughly speaking, the Principle of Sufficient Reason (PSR) states that everything must have a reason. If we construe PSR as entailing that the existence of everything has a cause (in the Avicennian sense explained earlier), then that a necessary existent has no cause is incompatible with PSR. The account that I have defended so far is therefore not based on PSR in its general form. It is nevertheless undeniable that we have no option but to embrace a weaker and arguably more compelling principle which applies only to the things whose existence is not necessary: every existent whose existence is not necessary in itself has a cause.[59] This principle – hereinafter called 'PSR*' – has a pivotal function throughout all of Avicenna's discussions regarding the existence of God.

Although a necessary existent has no cause, its existence is not a brute fact in the sense that it has no explanation or reason. It can be said that a necessary existent exists *because* its nature or essence is such that it cannot not exist. So the existence of a necessary existent has an explanation, even though it is not ontologically dependent on anything.[60] We can provide an answer for the question of why such a thing exists despite the fact that its existence is

---

[59] Avicenna's commitment to this principle can straightforwardly be concluded from (2005, chap. I.6, sec. 4) where he says: 'whatever is possible in existence when considered in itself, its existence and non-existence are both due to a cause'.

[60] This is a view I share with McGinnis (2010a, p. 170) and Richardson (2014, p. 756, n. 45).

groundless in the technical sense introduced earlier.[61] This of course does not stop us from pushing the question further and asking why it is the case that the essence of some things is such that they cannot not exist while the essence of some other things is such that they can not exist. In other words, the whole idea of the modal distinction could be challenged. Many Avicenna scholars seem to believe that the modal distinction cannot be justified unless we appeal to an application of one or another interpretation of PSR.[62] Making this claim precise, I argue that PSR* is exactly the principle we require to defend the modal distinction expressed by the following proposition:

(A) For every existent O, either O is necessary in itself or O is possible in itself but necessary through another.

To capture the role PSR* plays in justifying A, consider the following proposition, which is logically true:

(B) For every existent O, either O is uncaused, or O is caused by itself, or O is caused by something other than itself.

We have argued that there can be no self-caused existent. Indeed, it seems that *causation* must by definition be an irreflexive notion. This rules out the possibility that something can be caused by itself. Accordingly, B is logically equivalent to the following proposition:

(C) For every existent O, either O is uncaused, or O is caused by something other than itself.

If O is caused by something other than itself, then the existence of O depends on the existence of its cause. Thus, O's existence is not necessary in itself; it is merely possible in itself and must be necessitated through its cause. This indicates that the second disjunct of C entails the second disjunct of A. On the other hand, if we accept PSR*, the first disjunct of C would similarly entail the first disjunct of A. This is because, if it is true that every existent whose existence is not necessary in itself has a cause, then an uncaused existent must

---

[61] For those who are familiar with reformed epistemology, the issue at stake can better be understood by resorting to a comparison. Plantinga (in (1981, 1983) and many other places) argues that our basic beliefs – based on which all our other beliefs are justified, either directly or, at least, indirectly – are neither self-justified nor justified through other beliefs and propositions. Nevertheless, they have an epistemic ground. More precisely, it is explicable why we can hold those beliefs without violating our epistemic duties. Similarly, we can say that the Necessary Existent – by which all other existents are caused, either directly or at least indirectly – is neither self-caused nor caused by any other thing. Nevertheless, its existence is not a brute fact for which we have no explanation. Note that the epistemic sense of grounding to which Plantinga appeals should not be confused with the ontological sense of grounding discussed earlier.

[62] See, among others, Bäck (1992) and Richardson (2014).

be a necessary existent. In consequence, if O is uncaused, then O is necessary in itself. So each of the disjuncts of C entails the corresponding disjunct of A, provided that PSR* is true. This means that the conjunction of C and PSR* entails A. More precisely, the modal dichotomy expressed by A can be justified by the conjunction of B (which expresses a logical truth), the irreflexivity of causation (which is in some sense concealed in the definition of this notion), and PSR*.

Moreover, if O is necessary in itself, then there is neither any condition whose satisfaction is necessary for the existence of O, nor any circumstances in which O fails to exist. This indicates that the essence of O must be such that O cannot not exist. On the other hand, if O is possible in itself but necessary through another thing – say through X – then O's existence depends on the existence of X. Hence, the existence of X is a condition whose satisfaction is necessary for the existence of O. If X does not exist, O fails to exist too. This indicates that the essence of O must be such that O can not exist. These observations yield that, if we accept that every existent has an essence, then D can easily be concluded from A:

(D) For every existent O, either the essence of O is such that O cannot not exist or the essence of O is such that O can not exist.

Recall that this discussion was initiated due to the potential doubts which could be raised concerning the plausibility of D. Now it is established that D can be concluded from the conjunction of B (which expresses a logical truth), PSR*, and a few innocent assumptions – that is, the irreflexivity of causation and that every existent has an essence. This should relieve us of our concerns that D might be unjustified.

In sum, it seems that we have to accept a weak version of PSR – that is, PSR* – according to which every existent whose existence is not necessary in itself has a cause. We do not need any version of PSR that is stronger than PSR*, either for justifying the Avicennian modal distinction or for defending Avicenna's arguments for the existence of at least one necessary existent. Now it is time to see how these arguments work.

4 The Existence of a Necessary Existent

Over the course of this section, I reconstruct four arguments for the existence of at least one necessary existent. Three of the arguments can be extracted from Avicenna's own texts, or so I argue. The first argument, which is probably the least sophisticated and the most controversial, has striking affinities with the ontological argument proposed by Alvin Plantinga. The second argument presupposes, first, that every existent that is possible in itself is caused and, second, that every such possible thing coexists with its cause. It can be shown that the conjunction of these claims implies that no possible thing can exist unless there is a necessary existent in the chain of its causal predecessors. The general structure of the third argument resembles that of the well-known cosmological arguments (e.g., the Kalām Cosmological Argument (KCA)), one of whose premises is the impossibility of the existence of actual infinites. The fourth argument is reconstructed based on the most popular interpretation of the Proof of the Sincere and, like the first two arguments, does not rely on the impossibility of actual infinities. In the last subsection of this section, I turn to the issue of whether these arguments are ontological.

4.1 A Plantingean Argument

In his scrutiny of Avicenna's argument for the existence of God, McGinnis states: 'I should say that I find nothing like an Anselmian ontological-style argument for the existence of God in Avicenna. Consequently, I think that the question of whether there is anything necessary through itself is for Avicenna a genuinely open one.'[63] I agree with McGinnis to the extent that I concede that no ontological-style argument can be found in Avicenna's works which he himself counts as an independent and self-standing argument for the existence of God. Nonetheless, there are passages in Avicenna's works in which his reasoning bears a close resemblance to some well-known ontological arguments – for example, that of Plantinga. Consider the following excerpt with which the second chapter of the metaphysics part of *The Salvation* begins:

> The necessary existent is the existent which if hypothesized to be non-existent an absurdity follows. The possible existent is that which if hypothesised to be non-existent or existent no absurdity follows.[64]

Avicenna mentions these phrases to introduce the modal dichotomy between necessary and possible things. However, we can also detect the main premise of an ontological argument in the first sentence of the passage. If the non-existence of a necessary existent is by definition logically absurd, then it would be obvious

---

[63] McGinnis (2010a, p. 164).

[64] Avicenna (1985, p. 546), my translation. It is worth highlighting that the use of 'the' in the phrase 'the necessary existent' should not be hastily taken as evidence that Avicenna has presupposed that there can be only one necessary existent. Otherwise, based on a similar observation – that is, that he has used 'the' in 'the possible existent' – we would have to accept that he believes that there can be only one possible existent. But we know that he does not believe that. As a result, in the text just cited, 'the necessary existent' and 'the possible existent' must be read as indefinite descriptions which can in principle apply to more than one thing. So the text can be paraphrased like this: a necessary existent is an existent which if hypothesised to be non-existent an absurdity follows. A possible existent is that which if hypothesised to be non-existent or existent no absurdity follows. See also the translation offered by McGinnis and Reisman (2007, p. 211).

that that necessary existent exists. Accordingly, if we understand God to be a necessary existent, as Avicenna certainly does, then it is logically impossible that God does not exist. It is quite reasonable to take this passage as witnessing that, for Avicenna, the non-existence of God is logically impossible. That is why William Lane Craig understands this passage as anticipating the ontological arguments later proposed by Anselm and others.[65] Indeed, Avicenna could have complemented the first sentence as follows:

> The necessary existent is the existent which if hypothesised to be non-existent an absurdity follows. God is a necessary existent. Therefore, God exists.

But since Avicenna did not do so, we are not justified to assume that he himself takes the quoted passage as presenting an independent argument for the existence of God as a necessary existent.[66] However, it still seems fairly defensible that an ontological argument can be reconstructed based on the quoted text. Such an argument would run as follows:

Argument A1
1. God is a necessary existent in itself (definition).
2. A necessary existent in itself cannot not exist (definition).
3. God cannot not exist (from 1 and 2).
4. God does not exist (*reductio* assumption).
5. God can not exist (from 4).
6. Contradiction: God cannot not exist and God can not exist (from 3 and 5).

Therefore:

7. God exists (from 4–6).

According to this argument, if we understand God as an existent whose existence, unlike the existence of ordinary things that we know, does not depend on any other thing and is therefore necessary in Itself, then the denial of God's existence expresses a logical impossibility. The only step of *Argument A1* which might need some elucidation is the move to line 5 from line 4. This step is based on the fact that truth entails possibility. Avicenna believes that if something is true at a time, then it is a fortiori possible. This principle is also acceptable in most of the well-known modern systems of modal logic – more precisely, in all systems where the accessibility relation in their possible-world semantics is reflexive. In such a system, the truth of a proposition in a possible world w implies the truth of that proposition in a possible world (i.e., w itself) which

---

[65] Craig (1980, p. 87).

[66] For the same reason, Craig (1980, pp. 87–8) and Zagzebski (2007, p. 48, n. 35) do not consider Avicenna the inventor of the ontological arguments.

is accessible from *w*. Hence the truth of a proposition in *w* implies its possibility in this world. This reassures us that concluding 5 from 4 is unproblematic.

An immediate objection to which *Argument A1* might be prone is that the notion of *necessary existent* or, more specifically, the notion of *necessary existent in itself*, is not a logically consistent notion. If this is true, then not only God's existence but also any other thing, including God's non-existence, can be concluded from the premise that God is a necessary existent in itself. Stated otherwise, by assuming that God possesses a self-contradictory property, we can prove anything we want about God. As a result, *Argument A1* fails to establish the actual existence of God. For Avicenna, however, this criticism is a non-starter. This is because Avicenna excludes things whose existence is impossible in itself from the outset. In fact, the distinction between (1) necessary in itself and (2) possible in itself but necessary through another is made only among the things whose existence is not impossible in itself.[67] Avicenna's entire discussion of the modal distinction can be seen as a defence of the possibility or self-consistency of the notion of *necessary existence*. It is only after knowing that something *can* exist that we ask whether it is also the case that that thing *can not* exist. Necessary existence is a property attributable only to some of those things which can exist. So this property is in principle instantiable, and its corresponding notion – that is, the notion of *necessary existent* – is by definition self-consistent.

Viewed from this angle, we can see that, given the Avicennian conception of a necessary existent, the mere fact that there *can in principle be* a necessary existent would entail that there *is* a necessary existent. This is exactly the main insight behind Plantinga's ontological argument.[68] Employing the Avicennian terminology of 'necessary existent in itself', we can reformulate the least complicated version of Plantinga's argument as follows:

Argument A2

1. There can be a necessary existent in itself.

Therefore:

2. There is a necessary existent in itself.

The first premise of the argument affirms that the property of necessary existence is instantiable and there is no inconsistency in the assumption that

---

[67] See the second passage quoted in subsection 3.4.

[68] This ontological argument is defended in Plantinga (1974, 1977), among other places. The succinct presentation of *Argument A2* is inspired by Bohn (2017, sec. 3.1) and Pruss and Rasmussen (2018, sec. 2.4). For a recent discussion of the subtleties of Plantinga's argument, see Rasmussen (2018).

something possesses this property. But the existence of a necessary existent is not conditional on anything. A necessary existent is by definition uncaused, and its existence neither hinges on the realisation of anything in the world nor can be hindered by anything. If there *can be* a being that needs no cause and whose existence nothing can prevent, then it would be undeniable there *is* such a being. Thus conclusion 2 can be validly derived from premise 1. This Avicennian strategy for establishing the validity of *Argument A2* differs from the standard Plantingean approach, which is based on possible-world semantics. According to the first premise of *Argument A2*, it is true in the actual world that there can be a necessary existent. This entails that there is a possible world *w*, accessible from the actual world, in which there is a necessary existent. Suppose that G is a necessary existent inhabitant of *w*. Since the existence of G is necessary, it must exist in all the possible worlds which are accessible from *w*. Now if the system of modal logic we are working with is such that the accessibility relation of its possible-world semantics is symmetric, then the accessibility of *w* from the actual world implies the accessibility of the actual world from *w*. So the existence of a necessary existent like G in *w* entails the existence of G in the actual world and this proves the conclusion of *Argument A2*. Moreover, the symmetricity of the accessibility relation holds in S5, which is not only Plantinga's favourite modal logic but also arguably the most popular system among analytic metaphysicians in general. This reassures us that *Argument A2* enjoys a consensus concerning its validity, even though there could be disagreement about the truth of its premise.[69]

Argument A1, compared to *Argument A2*, is more straightforwardly built upon Avicennian insights. But *Argument A2* aims at a more modest conclusion. It merely intends to show that there is *at least* one necessary existent, without making any claim about whether there is *only* one necessary existent or whether God exists. In this respect, *Argument A2* is similar to the arguments discussed in the next three subsections.

4.2 Argument from Necessitation

In his discussion of the modal distinction in chapter I.6 of *The Metaphysics of The Healing*, Avicenna provides a detailed explanation of why a necessary existent inevitably appears in the chain of the causal ancestors of every

---

[69] Despite his general scepticism about the plausibility of labelling Avicenna's argument for the existence of God as an ontological argument, McGinnis (2010a, pp. 169–70) has astutely noticed that important commonalities between Avicenna's approach and the Plantingean argument can be traced. See also Morewedge (1970, 1980) and Johnson (1984) for the attribution of more or less similar ontological arguments to Avicenna.

existent.[70] This explanation, which can be construed as an independent argument for the existence of at least one necessary existent, goes as follows:

> We thus say: [the possible in itself] must become necessary through a cause and with respect to it. For, if it were not necessary, then with the existence of the cause and with respect to it, it would [still] be possible. It would then be possible for it to exist or not to exist, being specified with neither of the two states. [Once again,] from the beginning this would be in need of the existence of a third thing through which either existence (as distinct from non-existence) or non-existence (as distinct from existence) would be assigned for [the possible] when the cause of its existence with [this state of affairs] would not have been specified. This would be another cause, and the discussion would extend to an infinite regress. And, if it regresses infinitely, the existence of the possible, with all this, would not have been specified by it. As such, its existence would not have been realized. This is impossible, not only because this leads to an infinity of causes – for this is a dimension, the impossibility of which is still open to doubt in this place – but because no dimension has been arrived at through which its existence is specified, when it has been supposed to be existing. Hence, it has been shown to be true that whatever is possible in its existence does not exist unless rendered necessary with respect to its cause.[71]

This passage spells out how the existence of a possible existent at root hinges on the existence of a necessary existent. More specifically, it sets out how no thing that is possible in itself can exist unless its existence is ultimately caused and necessitated by a necessary existent, perhaps through the mediation of a series of other existents which are again possible in themselves. An indispensable corollary of this line of reasoning is that the mere existence of even a single existent in the world – regardless of whether it is necessary or possible in itself – entails the existence of a necessary existent. A big advantage such an argument for the existence of a necessary existent can claim over some of its rivals is that it in principle avoids all questions to do with the impossibility of actual infinites. So even someone who is suspicious of the coherence of Aristotelian–Avicennian finitism might still be persuaded of the soundness of this argument. Let me explain how this can happen.

---

[70] For the sake of simplicity, here I assume that every existent has only one chain of causal ancestors. But if we accept the possibility of causal overdetermination – in the sense that an existent X might have more than one efficient cause each of which is sufficient to cause the existence of X – then it is in principle possible that an existent has more than one causal chain. In this case, we can apply the arguments of this and the following sections to a randomly chosen chain of the causal ancestors of that existent.

[71] Avicenna (2005, chap. I.6, sec. 6). Contrary to our practice in other passages from *The Metaphysics of The Healing*, the parentheses of this passage are by Marmura.

Consider an arbitrary existent O. If O is necessary in itself, then the desired result is already achieved. If O is not necessary in itself, then it is possible in itself and must have been necessitated through a cause distinct from itself. Now if the cause of O is necessary in itself, then we have arrived at the desired conclusion. Otherwise, the cause of O is itself a merely possible thing whose existence is necessitated through another cause. A similar line of argument can be repeated for the cause of the cause of O and for all the causal ancestors of O in general until we arrive at a necessary existent. To prove that the chain of the causal ancestors of O will definitely end in a necessary existent, we need to rule out two possibilities: (1) There might be a circle in the chain of the causal ancestors of O. (2) This chain might be extended infinitely without ever ending in a necessary existent.

If there is a circle in the chain of the causal ancestors of O, then in this chain there can be found an existent X which is causally linked to itself either directly or indirectly through the mediation of a series of existents like $X_1, X_2, \ldots, X_{n-1}$, and X_n such that X is caused by X_1, X_1 by X_2, ..., X_{n-1} by X_n, and X_n by X (Figure 1).[72] In the latter case, it follows from the transitivity of causation that X is ultimately caused by itself. So, if X is causally linked to itself, no matter if this link is direct or through some intermediary causes, then it must be considered as a self-caused existent. However, due to the irreflexivity of causation

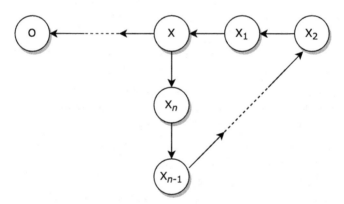

Figure 1 There cannot be a circle in the chain of the causal ancestors of an existent (e.g., O) because otherwise there would be an existent (e.g., X) that causes itself.

---

[72] Here '*n*' designates a natural number equal to or greater than 1.

no existent can be caused by itself.[73] This establishes that there can be no circle in the chain of the causal ancestors of O. So the first possibility is ruled out.

Now let us turn to the other possibility, according to which the chain of the causal ancestors of O might be extended infinitely without ever reaching a necessary existent. One tactic to refute this possibility is to employ arguments against the actual existence of an infinite number of elements. We pursue this approach in the next subsection; here we confine ourselves to arguments which are free from the assumption of finitism. Avicenna intends to sketch such an argument in the passage quoted, without explicitly mentioning all its hidden assumptions. The principle of the coexistence of cause and effect is one of those hidden assumptions, without which providing a finitism-free argument does not seem feasible. This principle ensures that O and all its causal ancestors must exist together simultaneously; if O exists at the present time, then the cause of O and the cause of the cause of O and so on must all similarly exist at the present time. But, on the other hand, if all the causal predecessors of O are merely possible in themselves, then none of them can be necessitated. In turn, O cannot be necessitated (or, equivalently, necessary through another) either. Put metaphorically, O awaits necessitation by its cause, the cause of O awaits necessitation by the cause of the cause of O, and so on. But since, by assumption, there is no necessary existent in the causal history of O, none of those waitings comes to an end; thus neither O nor any of its causal ancestors comes into existence.[74] This contradicts the initial assumption that O exists. Therefore, the possibility that the chain of the causal ancestors of O can regress infinitely without ever being stopped by a necessary existent must be false. Thus the second alternative we started from is ruled out too. Now we can safely conclude that for every arbitrary existent O, the chain of the causal predecessors of O must end in a necessary existent. This shows that the existence of even a single existent guarantees the existence of at least one necessary existent.

It is worth emphasising that the possibility of having an infinite regress of non-existential/non-essential (e.g., material) causes which exist in different moments or periods of time is left open by the argument just presented. If, as Avicenna believes, time has no beginning, then there can be infinite series of such causes extended from the infinite past to the present. For instance, it would be metaphysically possible that there was no first human being; if so, the chain

---

[73] Even if we had accepted the alternative interpretation that every self-caused existent is necessary in itself, then the argument developed here shows that X is a necessary existent. So we have a warrant for the existence of at least one necessary existent and the desired conclusion is reached.

[74] The use of the term 'history' could be misleading here because all causal ancestors of O exist at the same time.

of the ancestors of a human being who exists at the present time could in principle be infinite. There could be no first in the chain of her ancestors. This possibility is not something which can be repudiated by this argument.[75] Moreover, what the argument is intended to show is not primarily that the number of causal ancestors of O cannot be infinite; it is rather that the chain of its causal ancestors must end in a necessary existent, whether or not the number of the intermediary causes between that necessary existent and O is finite or infinite.[76] This text brings to our attention, once again, that if O is possible in itself, then its essence would be neutral with respect to existence and non-existence. So, if O exists, its existence must eventually be forced by a necessary existent. The mere extravagant proliferation of causal ancestors each of which is possible in itself cannot bring O any closer to existence, even if this proliferation is limitless and goes on infinitely. Increasing the number of merely possible things cannot make the existence of anything necessary. Using alternative terminology, it can be said that the existence of no ontologically dependent entity can be guaranteed just based on the presence of a chain of ontological ancestors every element of which is itself an ontologically dependent entity. Only the presence of an ontologically independent entity among the ancestors of an ontologically dependent entity can eventually satisfy the condition for the existence of the latter entity. This is a fact whose truth does not hinge on the number of the ontological ancestors of the entity under discussion.

This argument relies on a profound intuition which is captured by a slogan of the later Muslim philosophers: '*fāqid al-šay' lā-yakūnu mu'ṭī al-šay*' (what lacks something cannot give it). A series of ontologically dependent entities cannot bestow existence upon another thing, although they can transfer existence from an ontologically independent entity. This is because ontologically dependent entities do not possess existence on their own so they cannot be givers of existence either, or so the intuitively plausible slogan tells us. In the parallel framework, a chain of things all of which are possible in themselves cannot necessitate (or give necessity to) the existence of another thing. This is because necessity is exactly what they lack, even though their number is infinite. The necessity of existence must be given, either directly or indirectly, by a necessary existent.

---

[75] Avicenna's belief in the eternity of the past was criticised by al-Ġazālī. He argues that this doctrine entails that the number of people who have lived so far and, correspondingly, the number of human souls, is infinite. But this, al-Ġazālī contends, is in tension with Avicenna's rejection of the existence of actual infinites. On this, see Marmura (1960), McGinnis (2010b), and Zarepour (2020b, sec. 4.3).

[76] To be clear, I do not claim that Avicenna allows the existence of an infinite number of intermediary causes. I rather contend that the argument in question, as I reconstructed it, is based on no specific assumption regarding the number of intermediary causes.

In general, if there is no necessary existent in the world, then nothing could be necessitated either. But if something exists, then its existence is either necessary in itself or necessitated through another thing. So, if something exists, then a necessary existent exists too. The heart of this argument lies in what I call the Necessitation Principle. This principle states that if an existent is possible in itself but necessary (or, equivalently, necessitated) through another, then there must be a necessary existent in the chain of its causal ancestors. Embedding this principle as one of the premises of our finitism-free argument, we can capture its general structure as follows:

Argument B

1. Something – call it 'O' – exists (assumption).
2. Either O is necessary in itself or O is possible in itself but necessary (or necessitated) through another (from 1 and the modal distinction).
3. If O is necessary in itself, then there is a necessary existent (self-evident).
4. If O is possible in itself but necessary (or necessitated) through another, then there must be a necessary existent among the causal ancestors of O (from the Necessitation Principle).
5. If O is possible in itself but necessary (or necessitated) through another, then there is a necessary existent (from 4).

Therefore:

6. There is a necessary existent (from 2, 3, and 5).

Since *Argument B* is based on the modal distinction which is in turn justified by appealing to PSR*, the soundness of this argument depends on PSR*. Moreover, *Argument B* relied on the irreflexivity and transitivity of causation because the justification of the Necessitation Principle was partially based on them. But this argument is independent from the impossibility of actual infinities as well as the claim that every collection of possible existents is itself an existent which is either necessary in itself (i.e., uncaused) or necessitated through (i.e., caused by) another thing.[77] These latter claims play pivotal roles, respectively, in the next two arguments with which I engage.

4.3 Argument from Finitism

In the passage quoted at the beginning of the preceding subsection, we saw that Avicenna claimed that the chain of the causal predecessors of an existent which

---

[77] Pursuing an approach like mine, Cohoe (2013) shows that the first three of Aquinas' five ways of demonstrating the existence of God can be construed as having no dependency on the two aforementioned claims.

is possible in itself cannot be infinitely extended without ever reaching a necessary existent. He seems to believe that this claim is true for two distinct reasons. Having examined the second reason in the previous subsection, it is time to address the first, which is based on the impossibility of actual infinities.[78] An argument based on finitism for the existence of at least one necessary existent can be structured as follows:

Argument C

1. Something – call it 'O' – exists (assumption).
2. Either O is necessary in itself or O is possible in itself but necessary through another (from 1 and the modal distinction).
3. If O is necessary in itself, then there is a necessary existent (self-evident).
4. If O is possible in itself but necessary through another, then the chain of the causal ancestors of O is either circular or linearly infinite or linearly finite (self-evident).
5. The chain of the causal ancestors of O cannot be circular (from the irreflexivity and transitivity of causation).
6. If the chain of the causal ancestors of O is linearly infinite, then there can be an infinite collection of ordered things all of which coexist together and simultaneously (from the definition of causation and the principle of coexistence of cause and effect).
7. There cannot be an infinite collection of ordered things all of which coexist together and simultaneously (the impossibility of infinites).
8. The chain of the causal ancestors of O cannot be linearly infinite (from 6 and 7).
9. If O is possible in itself but necessary through another, then the chain of the causal ancestors of O is linearly finite (from 4, 5, and 8).
10. If the chain of the causal ancestors of O is linearly finite, then there is a necessary existent (from definitions).
11. If O is possible in itself but necessary through another, then there is a necessary existent (from 9 and 10).

Therefore:

12. There is a necessary existent (from 2, 3, and 11).

To see why this argument is valid, some of its premises need to be clarified. In premise 4, 'linearly' must be taken to be synonymous with 'non-circularly'. It is

---

[78] The argument propounded in *Al-Risāla al-'aršīya* is based on the impossibility of actual infinities. However, I prefer not to quote that argument here because the authenticity of this work – as Gutas (2014, pp. 484–5) has observed – is yet to be verified. For translations of this argument, see Hourani (1972, pp. 76–8) and Marmura (1980, pp. 144–5).

logically true that the chain of the ancestors of O is either circular or non-circular (i.e., linear). If it is non-circular, then it would be either finite (i.e., linearly finite) or infinite (i.e., linearly infinite). Premise 5 was justified in the previous subsection. The circularity of the chain of the ancestors of O, coupled with the transitivity of causation, would imply the existence of a self-caused existent. But this contradicts the irreflexivity of causation. So the chain in question cannot be circular. To justify premise 6, it suffices to take two facts into consideration. First, a linear chain of the causal predecessors of an existent like O naturally forms an ordered collection of things. The cause of O is the first member of this collection, the cause of the cause of O is the second member of this collection, and so on. Second, the members of this collection exist all together and simultaneously. This is due to the principle of the coexistence of cause and effect. This principle ensures that all the elements of the chain of the causal ancestors of an existent exist simultaneously. These two observations jointly justify premise 6.

The cornerstone of *Argument C* is premise 7. It is of vital importance to note that this premise does not reject the existence of *every* infinite collection. Avicenna ingeniously considers two constraints for the collections of objects whose actual infinity must be denied. He argues that no infinite collection of objects can actually exist if it satisfies the following conditions: (1) Its members naturally are or can be ordered (the ordering condition). (2) All its members exist together at the same time (the coexistence condition). Avicenna emphasises these conditions because he thinks that the validity of his main argument against the actual impossibility of infinite collections of objects depends on the satisfaction of these conditions. The argument I am talking about is usually called the Mapping Argument. To see how this argument works, suppose that S is an infinite collection of ordered objects. Now remove a finite number of the initial elements of S and call the remaining sub-collection S*. S and S* are both infinite and we can put them into a one-to-one correspondence by pairing the first element of S with the first element of S*, the second element of S with the second element of S*, and so on (Figure 2). But the one-to-one correspondence of S with one of its proper sub-collections – that is, S – entails a whole–part equality.[79] But such an equality is absurd, at least for a whole all of whose parts coexist simultaneously. Thus the existence of S – or, in general, the existence of any infinite collection whose elements are ordered and coexist at the same time – is impossible. It means that premise 7 is true.[80]

---

[79] X is a proper sub-collection of Y if every member of X is a member of Y but not vice versa.

[80] The subtleties of Avicenna's views regarding infinity are discussed by McGinnis (2010b) and Zarepour (2020b).

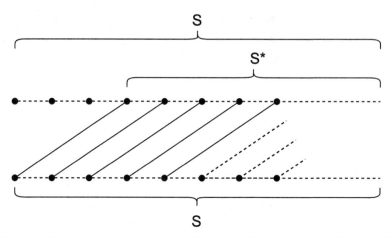

Figure 2 S is in one-to-one correspondence with its proper sub-collection S*.

The Mapping Argument cannot reject the existence of a temporal regress of, for example, events or material causes. For instance, it cannot show that the number of past sunrises till today is necessarily finite. Similarly, we cannot rule out the possibility of the existence of a human being whose chain of ancestors is linearly infinite. This is because neither of these collections satisfies the coexistence condition. All the past sunrises do not exist at the same time; nor do all the ancestors of a human exist at the same time. That is why, from an Avicennian perspective, the KCA is unsound. The advocates of the KCA employ the mapping technique to establish the finitude of the past. But from an Avicennian perspective, this application of the mapping technique is indefensible because there is obviously no infinite temporal regress of events or objects all of whose elements coexist at the same time.[81] In the same vein, we are unable to appeal to the Mapping Argument to refute the idea that there could be an infinite collection of objects whose elements cannot be ordered. If a collection does not satisfy the ordering condition, there is no standard strategy for pairing the elements of that collection with the elements of its sub-collections. So we cannot be sure we can put that collection in a one-to-one correspondence with at least one of its proper sub-collections, or so Avicenna has argued.

To complete our defence of *Argument C* we need to clarify why premise 10 is true. Suppose that the chain of the causal ancestors of O is linearly finite. Suppose that its length is n and it includes $X_1, X_2, \ldots, X_{n-1}$, and X_n such that O is caused by X_1, X_1 by $X_2, \ldots$, and X_{n-1} by X_n.[82] In this situation, X_n must be a necessary existent, otherwise X_n is possible in itself and must be necessitated

---

[81] The failure of the KCA in an Avicennian framework is shown by Zarepour (2021).

[82] Again, 'n' refers to a natural number equal to or greater than 1.

through another existent; there must be another element which causes X_n. If the element which causes X_n is identical to one of $X_1, X_2, \ldots, X_{n-1}$, and X_n, then the chain of the causal ancestors of O would be circular, not linear. So there must be another element X_{n+1} which causes X_n and is distinct from $X_1, \ldots, X_{n-1}$. If so, the length of the chain of the causal ancestors of O would be at least $n+1$. Since this contradicts our initial assumption, the horn that X_n is not a necessary existent must be false. Thus, it follows that if the chain of the causal ancestors of O is linearly finite, then there is a necessary existent.

This argument shows that every hierarchy of existents which are successively grounded in each other must be finite and end in a groundless fundamental being. This amounts to the claim that the mere existence of even a single existent entails the existence of at least one necessary existent. However, in addition to PSR*, the coexistence of cause and effect, and the irreflexivity and transitivity of causation, this argument also depends on the impossibility of a certain kind of infinite collection of objects (i.e., those whose elements are ordered and coexist together). Although Avicennian conservative finitism is more easily vindicated than the radical forms of finitism which absolutely reject the existence of any infinite collection of objects, it is still preferable to have, if possible, an argument which is free from even the conservative form of finitism. This is exactly what Avicenna seeks to do in *The Salvation*.

4.4 The Proof of the Sincere

Although the arguments presented in the previous two subsections can be (and indeed sometimes are) referred to as versions of the Proof of the Sincere, the most well-known version of this proof is arguably what Avicenna sets out in the metaphysics part of *The Salvation*. Like the other two arguments, the argument of *The Salvation* begins with the assumption that something – say, O – exists. If O is necessary in itself, then what we have sought is established. If, on the other hand, O is possible in itself, then consider the collection or totality of all the existents that are merely possible in themselves. The rest of the argument goes like this:

> Either the totality, inasmuch as it is that totality, exists – whether finitely or infinitely – necessarily in itself or possibly in itself. If the totality is necessary in itself while each of its parts is possible [in itself], then a necessary existent subsists through possible existents. But this is absurd. If the totality is possible in itself, then the totality needs for existence something [i.e., a cause] which bestows existence. So, [the cause] is either external or internal to the totality. If it [i.e., the cause] is internal to the totality, then it could be that [the cause is necessary in itself and, accordingly,] one of the parts of the totality is a necessary existent. But [it was assumed that] every one of them is

a possible existent. Thus, this is a contradiction. Or it could be that it is a possible existent and a cause of the existence of the totality. But a cause of the totality is *a fortiori* a cause of the existence of its parts (*aǧzāʾihā*), of which it [i.e., the cause] is one. Thus, it would be a cause of the existence of itself. [But this is impossible.] Despite its impossibility, if it were correct, it would have been, in a way, the desired conclusion. This is because everything that is sufficient to confer existence to itself is a necessary existent. But it was [assumed] not to be a necessary existent. This is a contradiction. What remains is that it [i.e., the cause] is external to it [i.e., the totality]. In this case, it cannot be a possible cause because we collected every cause that is a possible existent in this totality. So, this cause, being external to the totality, is necessary in itself.[83]

Avicenna considers the totality of all existents that are possible in themselves as an existent which must be either necessary or possible in itself. If this totality is necessary in itself, then the conclusion of the argument – that is, the existence of at least one necessary existent – is demonstrated. However, instead of accepting this claim, Avicenna prefers to insist that such a totality cannot be necessary in itself. He argues that a necessary existent cannot be identical to a collection of existents each of which is merely possible in itself. We will see in the next section that he argues that a necessary existent is purely simple and has no parts.[84] Thus the totality of all possible existents is merely possible in itself. Avicenna believes that the whole created world is an enormous, composed entity which could have not existed. If so, it must be necessitated through another existent. Suppose that the totality of the possible existents is T and it is caused by X. Since the existence of T in its totality depends on the existence of X, the existence of every member of T depends on X. This means that X is the cause of every single member of T. Now either X itself is a member of T, or it is not. If X belongs to T, then X would be the cause of itself. This is because, on one hand, X is the cause of every member of T and, on the other hand, X itself is a member of T. But this is absurd due to the irreflexivity of causation. So the cause of T cannot be one of its own members. Here, however, is one of those places where Avicenna apparently tolerates the reflexivity of causation. He says that even if we accept that X can be caused by itself, this means that X is a necessary existent. So what we are looking for has already been established. The only remaining option is that X is not a member of T. If this is the case, then X is definitely a necessary existent. This is because every existent that is

---

[83] Avicenna (1985, pp. 567–8), my translation. See also the translation offered by McGinnis and Reisman (2007, p. 215).

[84] Some contemporary philosophers have argued that even a complex totality composed of different parts can be necessary. To give an example, Vance (2020) argues that the whole world can be considered as a necessary being.

possible in itself belongs to T, which is the collection of *all* possible existents. This indicates that X, which falls outside T, is not possible in itself. It is therefore a necessary existent. Hence, there is at least one necessary existent. QED.

An immediate objection to which this argument might be vulnerable is that if, on one hand, T is the totality of the existents that are possible in themselves and, on the other hand, T itself can be considered as a possible existent whose existence is necessitated through another existent, then T would be a member of itself. Knowing about problems and controversies that can arise from the self-membership of a collection of things (e.g., the Russell paradox) warns us that T might create similar challenges. If we cannot define the totality in question in a way that it does not include itself, then the soundness of this argument could be jeopardised, or so the objector might complain. The easiest way to overcome this obstacle is to understand the relation between existents that are possible in themselves and T as a *parthood* relation instead of a *membership* relation. Indeed, in the aforementioned passage, Avicenna himself uses the Arabic term '*aǧzā*' whose most accurate translation in this context could be 'parts'. So T can be defined as a totality of which every existent that is possible in itself is a part. Put differently, we can conceive T as the mereological sum of all the existents that are possible in themselves. Since everything is a (non-proper) part of itself, T can be counted as a part of itself without triggering a problem.[85]

My formal reconstruction of this version of the Proof of the Sincere is founded on two premises with which we have not dealt in the arguments discussed so far. The first premise – which is not explicitly mentioned in the passage just quoted – can be articulated as stating that if we have a group of existents (which exist all together at the same time), then the mereological sum of these existents is itself an existent to which the modal distinction is applicable. This means that such a mereological sum is either necessary in itself or possible in itself but necessitated through another. I refer to this premise as the Composition Principle. One might question the credibility of this principle by suggesting that its endorsement is tantamount to committing the fallacy of composition, but I do not think that this objection has any force. The fallacy of composition arises when we infer that a property P is true of a whole from the fact that P is true of every part of that whole. Admittedly, the Composition Principle affirms the validity of an inference with a similar structure. It says that if every element of a collection of objects is an existent to which the modal distinction is applicable, then the mereological sum of these elements has the

---

[85] X is a proper part of Y if the former is a part of the latter but not vice versa. Equivalently, X is a proper part of Y if it is the case both that X is not identical to Y and that X is a part of Y.

same property and is in the same manner an existent to which the modal distinction is applicable. Nevertheless, a mere similarity between the structure of the inference validated by the Composition Principle and that of the inferences which suffer from the fallacy of composition does not make the Composition Principle fallacious. Whether an inference with such a structure is fallacious depends on the nature of the property P which is being predicated of the whole based on its predication to the parts. To see how this is possible, consider a huge red building (of the size of, for example, the Eiffel Tower) that is built of millions of tiny pieces of LEGO. If someone argues that this building is small because every part of it is small, then of course her argument would be fallacious. But if she argues that this building is red because every part of it is red, her argument is sound. And by no means does it seem that existence or, more precisely, being-an-existent-to-which-the-modal-distinction-is-applicable, is one of those problematic properties whose application of the whole cannot be concluded from its application to the parts without committing a fallacy; in fact, existence appears to be *the* most innocent property in this respect, and the burden rests on the opponent of the Composition Principle to show the contrary (though it does not seem that such a mission is possible at all).

The second premise which has a pivotal role in this version of the Proof of the Sincere but was not appealed to in the previous arguments describes the relation between a cause of a totality and the parts of that totality. In the passage under discussion here, Avicenna contends that 'a cause of the totality is *a fortiori* a cause of the existence of its parts'. However, I think that what we need is a weaker but, fortunately, more defensible premise, according to which the cause of a totality is the cause of only those parts of the totality that are possible in themselves. If one of the parts of a totality is necessary in itself, it has no cause at all. Therefore, neither the cause of the totality nor any other thing can be counted as the cause of the part whose existence is necessary in itself. The premise that I find plausible states that if X is both possible in itself and a part of Y, then every cause of Y is a cause of X. Put otherwise, if something causes Y, then it causes every part of Y that is not necessary in itself. If we accept that a whole causes all its parts (or, at least, all its parts that are possible in themselves), then this premise can easily be justified through the transitivity of causation. This is because if something causes a whole and the whole itself causes a part, then the transitivity of causation entails that that thing causes the part too. But even if we find the idea that a whole causes its parts problematic, we can still be content to accept the premise under consideration. This premise could be accepted even by someone who pursues a bottom-up approach to ontology in which a whole cannot cause its parts because the former has itself been built upon the latter.[86] Suppose that X is both possible in itself and a part of Y. Suppose moreover that Y itself is caused by Z. The existence of Y cannot be necessitated unless the existence of all its possible parts is necessitated. This is because if a part of Y fails to exist, then Y itself as a whole would fail to exist too. As a result, Z cannot necessitate the existence of Y without necessitating the existence of every part of Y (like X) that is possible in itself. Once the existence of Y is necessitated by Z, the existence of X and every other part of Y that is possible in itself is guaranteed as well. What bestows existence to a whole bestows existence to every single part of it that is possible in itself. We can therefore safely endorse the claim that the cause of a whole is the cause of every part of it that is possible in itself. From now on, I will refer to this premise as the Transfer Principle.

To shed some light on how this principle works, let me discuss a few examples. Suppose that 'E_1+E_2' refers to the mereological sum of two existents E_1 and E_2. If both of these existents are necessary in themselves, then E_1+E_2 has no cause and is therefore necessary in itself. This is because neither the existence of E_1 nor that of E_2 is conditional on anything. Accordingly, the existence of E_1+E_2 is not conditional on anything either. The reason for this is that the existence of the mereological sum of two things is nothing but the mere existence of those things. Since E_1 and E_2 cannot not exist, E_1+E_2 cannot not exist either.[87] Now suppose that E_1 is a necessary existent while E_2 is merely possible in itself. Since E_2 can fail to exist, so can E_1+E_2. This indicates that E_1+E_2, like E_2, is merely possible in itself. There must be a cause which necessitates its existence. Now suppose that C_2 is the cause that necessitates the existence of E_2. As soon as E_2 exists, so does E_1+E_2. This is because E_1 is, *ex hypothesi*, a necessary existent whose existence is not conditional on anything. The existence of E_1+E_2 is therefore conditional only on the existence of E_2, and since this condition can be satisfied by C_2, the cause of E_1+E_2 is C_2 itself. One might insist that this conclusion is absurd because it implies that C_2 is the cause of a necessary existent – that is, E_1. The objection is, however, untenable. Such an implication could stand only if we accept a principle which certifies that the cause of a whole is the cause of every part of it, regardless of whether that part is possible in itself. Avicenna did apparently endorse this

---

[86] It seems quite tenable that the existence of a whole should be explanatorily posterior to the existence of its parts. This clarifies why the whole cannot be considered as the cause of its parts. In his defence of the simplicity of the Necessary Existents in the metaphysics part of *The Salvation*, Avicenna (1985, p. 552, l. 11) explicitly mentions that 'the parts are essentially prior to the whole'.

[87] For reasons explained in the next section, there is only one necessary existent. Moreover, no necessary existent can be compounded of two or more parts. But since these claims are not yet justified, we cannot simply take them for granted in this section. Thus the discussion developed here is neutral with regard to these presuppositions.

principle, but, as I have said, this principle does not seem to be true and it must be replaced by the Transfer Principle, which is in a sense weaker but enjoys more intuitive plausibility. According to the latter principle, the cause of a whole is the cause of every part of it that is possible in itself. From the fact that E_1+E_2 is necessitated by C_2, we cannot conclude that C_2 is the cause of E_1; at least this is not something we are permitted to do based on the Transfer Principle. Even if the cause of E_2 is precisely E_1 – that is, if $C_2=E_1$ – then E_1 would be the cause of E_1+E_2. But this still does not mean that E_1 is the cause of itself. The Transfer Principle states that if E_1 is the cause of E_1+E_2, then the former would be the cause of every part of the latter that is possible in itself. Since E_1 is, *ex hypothesi*, a necessary existent, then it would only be the cause of the other part of E_1+E_2, which is E_2. Consider a totality which contains God and all the existents that are possible in themselves and created by God. By necessitating the existence of the existents that are possible in themselves, God necessitates the existence of the totality. Nevertheless, this does not mean that God is the cause of itself. The irreflexivity principle has taught us that, as a necessary existent, God has no cause. Finally, if both E_1 and E_2 are possible in themselves, then the mereological sum of their causes would be the cause of E_1+E_2. So, if C_1 and C_2 are, respectively, the causes of E_1 and E_2, then C_1+C_2 would be the cause of E_1+E_2. Here, it follows from the Transfer Principle that C_1+C_2 is the cause of both E_1 and E_2.

In making these clarifications we notice that Avicenna's argument suffers from certain imprecisions which must be refined. On one hand, talking about whether the totality of all possible existents has a cause does not make any sense unless we accept something like the Composition Principle. On the other hand, this principle legitimises the assumption of the existence of totalities that are possible in themselves but also have parts that are necessary in themselves. An example of such a totality is E_1+E_2, where E_1 and E_2 are respectively necessary and possible in themselves. Now consider the totality T which includes *all* the existents that are possible in themselves. Since E_1+E_2 is possible in itself, it must be included in T. If so, given the transitivity of the parthood relation, E_1 must be considered as a part of T. E_1 is a part of E_1+E_2, which is itself a part of T. So E_1 is a part of T. This amounts to the inclusion of a necessary existent in T. It is not the case that every necessary existent is external to T. Nor is it the case that nothing internal to T can be the cause of T. It is in principle possible that T is caused by a necessary existent like E_1 that is itself a part of T.[88] This of course

---

[88] Indeed, if God exists, He must be considered as a part of the totality of all existents that are possible in themselves. This is because even if God Himself is a necessary existent, compound existents, like God+Eiffel (i.e., the mereological sum of God and the Eiffel Tower), are merely possible in themselves and must be contained in the totality of all existents that are possible in themselves. This is what the seemingly innocent Composition Principle imposes. But if

does not jeopardise the final goal of the argument, which is to establish the existence of at least one necessary existent, but it at least persuades us that providing a formal reconstruction of the Proof of the Sincere is not as straightforward as it may seem at the outset. In particular, it seems more confusing than helpful to talk about whether the cause of T is internal or external to it. With these concerns in mind, I put forward the following formalisation for the last and most well-known version of the Proof of the Sincere:

Argument D

1. Something – call it 'O' – exists (assumption).
2. Either O is necessary in itself or O is possible in itself (from 1 and the modal distinction).
3. If O is necessary in itself, then there is a necessary existent (self-evident).
4. If O is possible in itself, then the totality – call it 'T' – of all existents that are possible in themselves exists (from the Composition Principle).[89]
5. If T exists, either T is necessary in itself or T is possible in itself (from the modal distinction).
6. If T is necessary in itself, then there is a necessary existent (self-evident).
7. If T is possible in itself, then there is an existent X which causes T (from PSR*).
8. If there is an existent X which causes T, either X is necessary in itself or X is possible in itself (from the modal distinction).
9. If X is necessary in itself, then there is a necessary existent (self-evident).
10. If X is possible in itself, then X is both a part of T and possible in itself (from 4).
11. If X is possible in itself, then X is the cause of itself (from 7, 10, and the Transfer Principle).
12. X is not the cause of itself (from the irreflexivity of causation).
13. X is not possible in itself (from 11 and 12).
14. If there is an existent X which causes T, X is necessary in itself (from 8 and 13).
15. If there is an existent X which causes T, then there is a necessary existent (from 9 and 14).
16. If T exists, there is a necessary existent (5, 6, 7, and 15).

God+Eiffel is a part of a totality, we can then conclude, based on the transitivity of the parthood relation, that God Himself is a part of that totality.

[89] More precisely, T includes all existents that are possible in themselves and exist all together at the same time with O. However, to avoid more complexities, I do not repeatedly emphasise the simultaneous existence of all parts of T.

Therefore:

17. There is a necessary existent (from 2, 3, 4, and 16).

Although *Argument D* is relatively long and might appear complicated, the logic behind it is very simple. Consider an arbitrary existent O. If O is necessary in itself, then the desired conclusion is established. If, on the other hand, O is possible in itself, then there is at least one existent that is possible in itself. The Composition Principle allows us therefore to conclude that there is a totality T of all existents that are possible in themselves. Once again, if T is necessary in itself, then we have arrived at the conclusion. Otherwise, T is merely possible in itself and must be caused by an existent like X. Now, employing the modal distinction for the third time, we can argue that either X is necessary in itself or it is only possible in itself. If the former is true, then the conclusion of the argument is established. But if the latter disjunct is true, then X would be a part of T. This is because according to the latter disjunct, X is possible in itself. So, collecting all the existents that are possible in themselves, T includes X as well. This means that X is a possible existent that is both a part and a cause of T. The Transfer Principle implies that X is the cause of itself (Figure 3). But this is absurd due to the irreflexivity of causation. So X cannot be possible in itself. In a nutshell, even if neither O nor T are necessary in themselves, the cause of T – that is, X – would still be necessary in itself. In any case, the simple fact that an arbitrary existent like O exists entails the existence of at least one necessary existent.

A strength of *Argument D* that is worthy of attention is that it does not rely on the claim that if a totality consists of existents each of which is possible in itself, then the whole totality is similarly possible in itself.[90] I agree with Avicenna that this claim is true. But I think that the existence of a necessary existent can be

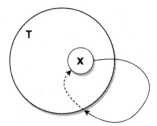

Figure 3 If X is both a part and a cause of X, it would be a cause of itself.

---

[90] Legenhausen (2005) has reconstructed the Proof of the Sincere in a way in which the aforementioned premise – according to which a complex entity whose every component is possible is itself possible – plays a crucial role.

proved even without resorting to this claim. All the arguments presented in this section are free from this assumption.

4.5 The Epistemological Status of the Arguments for the Existence of a Necessary Existent

Thus far, I have presented four different arguments for the existence of at least one necessary existent. Each of them, I believe, in one way or another can be taken as a construal of what is referred to in Avicenna scholarship as 'the Proof of the Sincere'. Admittedly, the further we move from *Argument A2* to *Argument D*, the greater could be the consensus on whether the reconstructed argument deserves that appellation; that is why I have used this title officially only for *Argument D*. To a large extent, the disagreements among Avicenna scholars over whether the Proof of the Sincere is an ontological argument stem from differences over what they take to be the correct reconstruction of this proof.[91] Everyone would accept *Argument A2* as an ontological argument. Although I would not find it surprising were Avicenna scholars to resist the idea that *Argument A2* can authentically be attributed to Avicenna, I believe, for the reason explained earlier, that the core insight behind this argument can be easily extracted from Avicenna's own texts.

Determining whether the other three arguments (i.e., *Argument B*, *Argument C*, and *Argument D*) are ontological or cosmological is more tricky and more sensitive to the subtleties of the exact definitions we consider for these types of arguments. For this reason, I prefer not to engage with the details of this issue here. Nevertheless, I emphasise that there is nothing a posteriori in these three arguments. *If* the notion of *being-an-ontological-argument* can be cashed out in terms of *having-purely-a-priori-premises*, then these three arguments can be categorised as ontological arguments. From an Avicennian perspective, all the key notions of these arguments – for example, *existence*, *causation* (albeit understood in the sense of ontological grounding), and the modal notions – can be grasped in an a priori manner, which means independently from all the information we may receive through our sense-perceptual experiences of the extramental world. Moreover, none of the essential principles on which these arguments are based needs to be justified by appeal to a posteriori data. Even PSR*, which may at first glance seem to rely on our observations of the outside world, is for Avicenna a purely rationalistic and a priori principle. If something

---

[91] For instance, Morewedge (1970) and Johnson (1984) believe that Avicenna's argument is ontological. Davidson (1987, chap. IX), on the other hand, considers it as a cosmological argument. Mayer (2001) and McGinnis (2010a, chap. 6) take this argument to be of a hybrid nature which in spite of having some ontological elements cannot be reconstructed as a purely ontological argument like that of Anselm.

is merely possible in itself, then it has perfectly equal degrees of inclination towards existence and non-existence. We do not need to appeal to experimental data to accept that in the absence of a cause, such an ideal balance will never be disrupted and neither existence nor non-existence will ever preponderate over the other. Focusing on the meticulous picture that Avicenna draws of the distinction between things that are necessary in themselves and things that are merely possible in themselves makes clear that PSR*, or at least a principle closely similar to it, is rooted in our a priori intuitions about existence. Finally, even the premise 'something exists', which is shared by all three of the arguments under consideration, can be justified a priori.[92] This premise can be concluded from the proposition 'I exist' and Avicenna, like many well-known contemporary analytic philosophers, believes that the latter proposition is a priori since it can be known even by the Flying Man who has no sense-perceptual experience and no access to experimental data.[93] In sum, it seems that there is nothing a posteriori in the Avicennian arguments for the existence of at least one necessary existent. Thus, *if* the only criterion for an argument to be ontological is its a priority, then we can safely put the Avicennian arguments on the list of ontological arguments.

It should be borne in mind that for Avicenna a priority is not synonymous with innateness. This is the case, at least, if we understand an innate piece of knowledge as something we know from birth. We do not gain innate notions after birth; they are within us from the beginning. If so, a priority does not necessarily entail innateness, though the other way around does hold. If we know something from birth, then obviously that thing is independent from any experimental data that we receive through our sense perceptions as we grow up. But there are many kinds of knowledge that we can grasp after birth yet in an a priori manner.[94] So the fact that Avicennian arguments for the existence of a necessary existent are a priori does not mean that they are innately known.

Before wrapping up this section, I would like to highlight a significant general conclusion that we can draw from the combination of the four arguments presented in this section. The last three arguments (i.e., *Argument B*, *Argument C*, and *Argument D*) share a general structure which can be summarised as follows:

---

[92] On the differences between the a priority of concepts/notions, judgements/propositions, and justifications/proofs, and on some of their consequences for Avicenna's philosophy, see Zarepour (2020a).

[93] The a priority of the proposition expressed by 'I exist' can be extracted from discussion of the semantics of indexicals as developed by, among others, Kaplan (1979) and Kripke (1980).

[94] Indeed, for Avicenna, even if the proposition expressed by 'I exist' is not innate, it can be grasped a priori after birth. On how this claim can be justified by a careful analysis of the Flying Man thought experiment, see Zarepour (2020c).

(a) Something exists.
(b) That thing is either necessary or possible in itself.
(c) If that thing is necessary in itself, then there is a necessary existent.
(d) If that thing is possible in itself, then (for reasons which vary from one argument to another) there is a necessary existent.

Therefore:

(e) There is a necessary existent.

Accordingly, if at least one of the three aforementioned arguments is sound, the following conditional claim is true:

(E) If something exists, then there is a necessary existent.

Or equivalently:

(F) If there is an existent, then there is a necessary existent.

It follows from F that:

(G) If there can be an existent, then there can be a necessary existent.

On the other hand, *Argument A2* tells us that:

(H) If there can be a necessary existent, then there is a necessary existent.

Now coupling G and H, we can conclude that:

(I) If there can be an existent, then there is a necessary existent.

So, if I am right and the arguments discussed in this section are sound, then the mere possibility of the existence of something, whatever it may be, entails the existence of at least one necessary existent. This is indeed an outstanding result, and much stronger than we expected. To establish the existence of a necessary existent, we do not need to presuppose even the *actual* existence of anything. The mere possibility that something *can* exist will lead us to the desired conclusion.

5 The Unity of the Necessary Existent

In the second section of this Element, I observed that Avicenna's theological programme is comparable to that of Anselm. Both identify a pivotal attribute for God and take the following steps: (a) They prove the existence of something which has that specific attribute. (b) They then put their efforts into extracting other divine attributes from that specific attribute. For Avicenna, the pivotal attribute of God is necessary existence. So far, reconstructing the Avicennian arguments, we have shown that there is at least one necessary existent. In an Avicennian framework, the latter result means that there is at least one God-like being. Now it is time to see how other divine properties that are traditionally attributed to God can be extracted from His being a necessary existent. The first two divine attributes that Avicenna tries to establish based on God's necessary existence are the uniqueness and simplicity of God. It is natural for a Muslim to follow this approach, as we remarked in the first section, because Islam is built upon the doctrine of *tawḥīd* and Muslim philosophers have interpreted the uniqueness and simplicity of God as two components of this doctrine: these components represent, respectively, the external and the internal unity of God. According to the external unity of God, there is only one being possessing divine attributes in general and necessary existence in particular. That is why God can be referred to by the definite description '*the* Necessary Existence'. On the other hand, God has also an internal unity in the sense that He is not divisible and has no internal part. God is perfectly simple (*basīṭ*). Thus God is One (*wāḥid*), both in the sense that He has no peer or partner and in the sense that he has no part. In the Avicennian framework, God has no peer and no part because He is not possible in itself. This is how monotheism and necessary existence are intertwined in this framework.

Avicenna usually discusses divine uniqueness before he turns to divine simplicity; sometimes, however, his argument for divine uniqueness consists of a sub-argument which he later uses to prove divine simplicity.[95] So, in a sense, the success of his argument for the uniqueness doctrine hinges on the success of his argument for the simplicity doctrine. In this section I address an argument for the uniqueness of the Necessary Existent which is not based on Its simplicity, but before going through the details of such an argument, let me first explain how we can prove that there is only one necessary existent based on the fact that no necessary existent can be compound (*murakkab*). Suppose that there are two distinct necessary existents N_1 and N_2. Since they both are necessary existent, there is at least one feature or property that they share. Call this feature N. On the other hand, since N_1 and N_2 are distinct from each other, each of them has at least one feature that the other lacks. Suppose that these distinguishing features of N_1 and N_2 are respectively X_1 and X_2. In other words, N_1 is compounded from N and X_1, and N_2 is compounded from N and X_2.[96] But this contradicts the assumption of the perfect simplicity of necessary existents. So, if it is true that every necessary

---

[95] This sub-argument is what Adamson (2013, pp. 177–81) calls 'the individuation argument'.

[96] One might bring to the picture the possibility that one of the two necessary existents can be constituted only from N and only the other has more than one component. Even if this can be the case, there is at

existent is simple, then the initial assumption that there can be more than one necessary existent is false. Given that we have already proved that there is at least one necessary existent, it follows that there is one and only one necessary existent. In the next subsection, I reconstruct an argument for the uniqueness of the Necessary Existent which does not rely on the assumption of the simplicity of all necessary existents.

5.1 There Is Only One Necessary Existent

In chapter IV.18 of his *Remarks and Admonitions*, Avicenna develops an argument for the uniqueness of the Necessary Existent whose core is summarised in the following phrases:

> The Necessary Existent is individuated (*al-muta 'ayyin*). If Its individuation is due to Its being a necessary existent, then there is no necessary existent other than It. And if Its individuation is not due to that [i.e., Its being a necessary existent] but to something else, then It is caused.[97]

We have proved that there is at least one necessary existent. Suppose that G is a necessary existent. G is an individuated being distinct from other existents. If G's individuation – that is, that G is the specific existent that it is – is due to its being a necessary existent, then there cannot be any necessary existent other than G. This is because if the individuation of G is solely due to its being a necessary existent, then being a necessary existent implies being that specific existent that G is. So, in a sense, every necessary existent is identical to G. Equivalently, there is only one necessary existent. What if the individuation of G is through something other than its being a necessary existent? Recall that the necessary existence is the essence of G as a necessary existent. That G cannot be completely individuated through its being a necessary existent therefore means that G cannot be individuated solely through its essential features. Consequently, G must have some accidental features which play ineliminable roles in its individuation. These accidental features must be conferred upon G by another thing. Otherwise, they are not accidental at all. Put differently, if those individuating features are bestowed upon G through its own essence (i.e., because of having the specific essence it has), then they would be essential to G rather than accidental. But we have supposed, on this horn, that the individuation of G is not through its essence and essential features. Now if

---

least one necessary existent that is not simple. This is not acceptable, however, because we have supposed that every necessary existent is simple.

[97] Avicenna (1957, chap. IV.18, vol. 3, p. 36), my translation. For a similar argument presented in *The Metaphysics of* The Healing, see Avicenna (2005, chap. I.6, secs. 7–13). The argument of *The Salvation* for the uniqueness of the Necessary Existent appears in Avicenna (1985, pp. 549–51).

we accept that G is individuated through accidental features that are given to it by something other than itself, then G would not be an independent being. Its individuation is at root through another thing. So G is an ontologically dependent entity or, to use Avicenna's own terminology, a caused entity. This clashes with the assumption that G is a necessary existent. The individuation of G cannot be through anything other than its own essence. But if so, then there is no necessary existent other than G.[98] That is why we can talk about *the* Necessary Existent. This argument can be formalised as follows:

Argument E

1. There is a necessary existent. Call it 'G'.
2. Either the individuation of G is entirely due to its essence or it is at least partially due to its accidents.
3. If the individuation of G is entirely due to its essence, then every necessary existent (having the same essence as G) is identical to G.
4. If the individuation of G is at least partially due to its accidents, then G must have accidental properties that are conferred upon it through something other than itself.
5. If something has accidental properties that are conferred upon it through something other than itself, then that thing is not a necessary existent (it is supposed to be self-independent in all respects).
6. If the individuation of G is at least partially due to its accidents, then G is not a necessary existent (from 4 and 5).
7. The individuation of G is not even partially due to its accidents (from 1 and 6).
8. The individuation of G is entirely due to its essence (from 2 and 7).

Therefore:

9. Every necessary existent is identical to G (from 3 and 8).

Therefore:

10. There is only one necessary existent.

---

[98] My presentation of the second horn of the argument in which G is assumed to be individuated through something other than its own essence does not exactly correspond to what Avicenna himself puts forward in the sequel of chapter IV.18 of *Remarks and Admonitions*. Nevertheless, I believe that this simplified argument is not only sound but also in harmony with the foundational elements of Avicenna's metaphysics. My argument bears close similarities to what Hamri (2018, p. 167) offers in defence of the uniqueness of a completely independent entity. For a meticulous discussion of Avicenna's argument and its reception by al-Rāzī and al-Ṭūsī, see Mayer (2003).

We have seen previously that the existence of every single existent is at root dependent on the existence of a necessary existent. Now we see that there is only one necessary existent, which we can refer to as the Necessary Existent. Coupling these two observations, we conclude that the existence of all existents depends on the Necessary Existent. This, to a large extent, suffices for us to take the Necessary Existent to be identical to the traditional God of the Abrahamic religions. Identifying these two notions makes even more sense if we can also show that the Necessary Existent is simple.

5.2 The Necessary Existent Is Simple

In chapter IV.21 of *Remarks and Admonitions*, Avicenna presents the following argument for the simplicity of the Necessary Existent:

> If the essence (*ḏāt*) of the Necessary Existent is composed from two or more aggregated things, It would be necessitated through them. Then one of them or every one of them is prior (*qabl*) to the Necessary Existent; and the Necessary Existent subsists in it. So, the Necessary Existent is not divisible either in meaning (*ma 'nā*) or in quantity.[99]

This argument is quite simple. Suppose that the Necessary Existent is a compound entity and has some parts. The parts of a whole, regardless of whether the whole is necessary or possible in itself, have some sort of explanatory priority over the whole. This is because these are the parts of a whole that make it what it is. So the whole is at least partially dependent on every single part of itself. Now if a whole is not simple, it would have at least two proper parts (i.e., parts that are not identical to the whole). The dependency of such a whole on its proper parts is tantamount to its dependency on things other than itself. This indicates that such a whole cannot be self-independent. As a result, it is not a necessary existent either. Hence, the Necessary Existent, inasmuch as it is self-independent, is simple and has no parts.

Although this argument has a great deal of force, I do not find it as convincing as an alternative which can be reconstructed based on Avicenna's discussion in *The Metaphysics of* The Healing.[100] Suppose that the Necessary Existent has a proper part X. X cannot be necessary in itself – otherwise we have at least two necessary existents – but we have already proved that there is only one necessary existent. So X is possible in itself. Note that there is no vicious circle here because we have at least one

---

[99] Avicenna (1957, chap. IV.21, vol. 3, pp. 44–5), my translation. For an extended argument for divine simplicity presented in *The Metaphysics of* The Healing, see Avicenna (2005, chap. I.7, secs. 1–13). Another version of this argument is discussed in *The Salvation* (1985, pp. 551–3).

[100] Avicenna (2005, chap. I.7, secs. 1–13).

argument for the uniqueness doctrine – that is, *Argument E* – in which the simplicity of necessary existents is not presupposed. Now if X is possible in itself, then it could have not existed. So it must be necessitated through another thing. But X cannot be necessitated through the essence of the Necessary Existent (more precisely, it does not exist just due to what the essence of the Necessary Existent is). This is because otherwise X would be an essential feature of the Necessary Existent and could not fail to exist. However, if X is necessitated through something other than the essence of the Necessary Existent, then the Necessary Existent is dependent on the thing through which the existence of X is necessitated. This contradicts the assumption that the Necessary Existent is totally self-independent. So the *reductio* assumption is false and the Necessary Existent is perfectly simple, possessing no proper part.

To be precise about the hidden assumption of this argument, it is worth noting that the argument is based on the assumption that every part of an existent is itself an existent which is subject to the modal distinction. Formally, if Y is an existent to which the modal distinction is applicable, so is every single part of Y. It is because of this assumption – which I call the Decomposition Principle – that we are allowed to talk about whether the parts of a necessary existent are necessary or possible in themselves. The function of the Decomposition Principle, as its name implies, is the opposite of the function of the Composition Principle. But both are equally defensible. Employing the Decomposition Principle, we can formally reconstruct the aforementioned argument for the simplicity of the Necessary Existent as follows:

Argument F
1. There is a necessary existent G that has a proper part X (*reductio* assumption).
2. Either X is necessary in itself or X is possible in itself (from 1 and the Decomposition Principle).
3. If X is necessary in itself, then there is more than one necessary existent.
4. There is only one necessary existent (from *Argument E*).
5. X is not necessary in itself (from 3 and 4).
6. X is possible in itself (from 2 and 5).
7. Either X is essential to G or X is accidental to G.
8. If X is essential to G, it could not fail to exist and would be necessary in itself.
9. X is not essential to G (from 5 and 8).
10. X is accidental to G (from 7 and 9).

11. If X is accidental to G, it is necessitated through something other than G itself.

12. If X is necessitated through something other than G itself, then G depends on that thing.

13. G, as a necessary existent, does not depend on anything.

14. X is not accidental to G (from 11–13).

15. Contradiction: X is accidental to G and X is not accidental to G (from 10 and 14).

Therefore:

16. There is no necessary existent which has a proper part (from 1–15).

Therefore:

17. The only necessary existent – that is, the Necessary Existent – is simple (from 4 and 16).

Note that premise 8 is true because G is a necessary existent whose essence is identical to necessary existence. So, if something comes from the essence of G, it cannot not exist. Premise 11 is true because if X were necessitated through G, then – given that the essence of G is identical to its existence – X would have been necessitated through the essence of G.[101] This in turn means that X is essential to G rather than accidental. Thus, if X is accidental to G, it must be necessitated through something other than G.[102]

A significant corollary of this argument is that, ontologically speaking, all essential features of the Necessary Existent are identical to each other and to the essence of the Necessary Existent, which is necessary existence. It is also worth highlighting that the immateriality of the Necessary Existent can immediately be concluded from its simplicity. Every material entity has at least two components: form and matter. So, being perfectly simple, the Necessary Existent cannot be material. Admittedly, there are still many other divine attributes that must be derived from necessary existence in order to claim that the gap between the Necessary Existent and the traditional God of the Abrahamic religion is completely filled. Due to limited space, this goal cannot be achieved in this Element. Nevertheless, even by relying solely on what we have shown so far, it is undeniable

---

[101] The claim that a specific part of G is necessitated through the essence of G should not be interpreted as equivalent to the claim that G is the cause of a part of itself. This interpretation is incompatible with the irreflexivity of causation. What I mean by the claim that a part of G is necessitated through the essence of G is nothing more than the claim that G has that specific part due to having the essence it has. This is exactly what that part's being essential to G means.

[102] For a discussion of objections to Avicenna's account of the unity and simplicity of Necessary Existent by post-Avicennian philosophers, see Alwishah (2018).

that the Avicennian Necessary Existent has striking similarities with the God of Abrahamic religions in general and with the Islamic conception of a monotheistic God in particular. The Necessary Existent is unique (*wāḥid*), simple (*basīṭ*), uncaused, self-subsisting (*qayyūm*), self-independent (*ṣamad*), immaterial, and the ultimate ground of the existence of every other being.[103]

6 Conclusion

Avicenna believes that the central attribute of God is necessary existence. He first establishes the existence of at least one necessary existent. Then he takes the second step and proves that there cannot be more than one necessary existent. Avicenna believes that the Necessary Existent is identical to the God of Islam and that every single property that is attributed to God can be extracted from necessary existence. If this is true, the first two steps of Avicenna's project can be seen as a defence of the Islamic conception of monotheism. In the last subsection of Section 4, I showed that if the arguments set out in that section are sound, we can conclude that:

(I) If there can be an existent, then there is a necessary existent.

Now we can see that if the Avicennian arguments developed in this section are also true, then we are assured that:

(J) There cannot be more than one necessary existent.

The conjunction of the two propositions entails that:

(K) If there can be an existent, then there is one and only one necessary existent.

If we take the existence of one necessary existent as the existence of one God, in its Avicennian sense, then K would be equivalent to:

(L) If there can be an existent, then monotheism is true.

Were we to ask Avicenna why monotheism is true, his answer would be something like this: 'Because there can be an existent.' The truth of a very substantial metaphysical theory – that is, monotheism – can be derived from an extremely thin metaphysical claim – that is, the mere possibility of the existence of something. This is impressive, and it is only one of the many reasons for which Avicennian Necessary Existent theology deserves more attention from contemporary philosophers in general and from analytic philosophers of religion in particular.

---

[103] Now it must be clear that Avicenna's understanding of necessary existent starkly contrasts with the view of those contemporary metaphysicians who believe that there are infinitely many necessary existents (e.g., numbers, sets, propositions, etc.). For Avicenna there is only one existent that is necessary in itself. All other things, including mathematical objects, are merely possible in themselves. See Zarepour (2016) for Avicenna's view regarding the status of mathematical objects.

References

Acar, R. (2005) *Talking about God and Talking about Creation: Avicenna's and Thomas Aquinas' Positions*. Leiden: Brill.

Adamson, P. (2007) *Al-Kindī*. Oxford: Oxford University Press.

Adamson, P. (2013) 'From the Necessary Existence to God', in Adamson, P. (ed.) *Interpreting Avicenna: Critical Essays*. Cambridge: Cambridge University Press, pp. 170–89.

Adamson, P. (2016) *Philosophy in the Islamic World*. Oxford: Oxford University Press.

Adamson, P., and Benevich, F. (2018) 'The Thought Experimental Method: Avicenna's Flying Man Argument', *Journal of the American Philosophical Association*, 4(2), pp. 147–64.

Ahmed, S. (2016) *What Is Islam? The Importance of Being Islamic*. Princeton, NJ: Princeton University Press.

Alwishah, A. (2013) 'Ibn Sīnā on Floating Man Arguments', *Journal of Islamic Philosophy*, 9, pp. 49–71.

Alwishah, A. (2018) 'Suhrawardī and Ibn Kammūna on the Impossibility of Having Two Necessary Existents', in Gheissari, A., Walbridge, J., and Alwishah, A. (eds.) *Illuminationist Texts and Textual Studies: Essays in Memory of Hossein Ziai*. Leiden: Brill, pp. 115–34.

Avicenna (1957) *al-Išārāt wa-l-tanbīhāt bi-šarḥ al-Ṭūsī [Remarks and Admonitions: With Commentary by Tusi]*. Edited by S. Dunyā. Cairo: Dār al-maʿārif.

Avicenna (1959) *al-Šifā', al-Manṭiq, al-Maqūlāt*. Edited by G. Anawati, M. M. Al-Khudairi, F. Al-Ahwani, and S. Zāyid Cairo: al-Maṭbaʿa al-amīrīya.

Avicenna (1964) *al-Šifā', al-Manṭiq, al-Qiyās*. Edited by S. Zāyid. Cairo: al-Maṭbaʿa al-amīrīya.

Avicenna (1977) *al-Rīyaḍīyāt, al-Hindasa*. Edited by A. I. Sabra and A. Lotfi. Cairo: al-Hayʾa al-miṣrīya al-ʿāmma l-il-kitāb.

Avicenna (1985) *al-Naǧāt [The Salvation]*. Edited by M. T. Danišpažūh. Tehran: Entešārāt-e Dānešgāhe Tehrān.

Avicenna (2005) *The Metaphysics of* The Healing. Edited and translated by M. E. Marmura. Provo, UT: Brigham Young University Press.

Bäck, A. (1992) 'Avicenna's "Conception of the Modalities"', *Vivarium*, 30(2), pp. 217–55.

Benevich, F. (2020) 'The Necessary Existent (wāǧib al-wuǧūd)', in Shihadeh, A., and Thiele, J. (eds.) *Philosophical Theology in Islam: Later Ashʿarism East and West*. Leiden: Brill, pp. 123–55.

Bennett, K. (2017) *Making Things Up*. Oxford: Oxford University Press.

Bertolacci, A. (2012) 'The Distinction of Essence and Existence in Avicenna's Metaphysics: The Text and Its Context', in Opwis, F., and Reisman, D. (eds.) *Islamic Philosophy, Science, Culture, and Religion: Studies in Honor of Dimitri Gutas*. Leiden: Brill, pp.257–88.

Bishop, J. (2007) *Believing by Faith: An Essay in the Epistemology and Ethics of Religious Belief*. New York: Clarendon.

Blackburn, S. (1984) *Spreading the Word: Groundings in the Philosophy of Language*. Oxford: Oxford University Press.

Bliss, R. (2014) 'Viciousness and Circles of Ground', *Metaphilosophy*, 45(2), pp. 245–56.

Bliss, R. (2018) 'Grounding and Reflexivity', in Bliss, R., and Priest, G. (eds.) *Reality and Its Structure: Essays in Fundamentality*. Oxford: Oxford University Press, pp. 70–90.

Bohn, E. D. (2017) 'Divine Necessity', *Philosophy Compass*, 12(11), pp. 1–10.

Bohn, E. D. (2018a) 'Against Hamri's Argument for the Ultimate Ground of Being', *International Journal for Philosophy of Religion*, 84(2), pp. 233–6.

Bohn, E. D. (2018b) 'Divine Foundationalism', *Philosophy Compass*, 13(10), pp. 1–11. http://doi.org/10.1111/phc3.12524

Burrell, D. B. (1993) *Freedom and Creation in Three Traditions*. Notre Dame, IN: University of Notre Dame Press.

Cohoe, C. (2013) 'There Must Be a First: Why Thomas Aquinas Rejects Infinite, Essentially Ordered, Causal Series', *British Journal for the History of Philosophy*, 21(5), pp. 838–56.

Cole, J. (2019) 'Paradosis and Monotheism: A Late Antique Approach to the Meaning of Islām in the Quran', *Bulletin of the School of Oriental and African Studies*, 82(3), pp. 403–25.

Correia, F. (2008) 'Ontological Dependence', *Philosophy Compass*, 3(5), pp. 1013–32.

Corrigan, K. (1996) 'Essence and Existence in the Enneads', in Gerson, L. P. (ed.) *The Cambridge Companion to Plotinus*. Cambridge: Cambridge University Press.

Craig, W. L. (1980) *Cosmological Argument from Plato to Leibniz*. London: Macmillan.

Cresswell, M. J. (1971) 'Essence and Existence in Plato and Aristotle', *Theoria*, 37(2), pp. 91–113.

Cupitt, D. (1984) *The Sea of Faith*. Cambridge: Cambridge University Press.

Davidson, H. A. (1987) *Proofs for Eternity, Creation and the Existence of God in Medieval Islamic and Jewish Philosophy*. Oxford: Oxford University Press.

Deng, D.-M. (2020) 'A New Cosmological Argument from Grounding', *Analysis*, 80(3), pp. 418–26.

Diller, J. (2019) 'Being Perfect Is Not Necessary for Being God', *European Journal for Philosophy of Religion*, 11(2), pp. 43–64.

Donner, F. M. (2019) 'Dīn, Islām, und Muslim im Koran', in Tamer, G. (ed.) *Die Koranhermeneutik von Günter Lüling*. Berlin: De Gruyter, pp. 129–40.

Euclid (1908) *The Thirteen Books of Euclid's Elements*. Translated by T. L. Heath. Cambridge: Cambridge University Press.

Evans, C. S. (1998) *Faith beyond Reason: A Kierkegaardian Account*. Grand Rapids, MI: Eerdmans.

Fine, K. (2001) 'The Question of Realism', *Philosophers' Imprint*, 1(2), pp. 1–30.

Franklin, M. F. (1993) 'The Indispensability of the Single-Divine-Attribute Doctrine', *Religious Studies*, 29(4), pp. 433–42.

Gutas, D. (2014) *Avicenna and the Aristotelian Tradition*. Second Ed. Leiden: Brill.

De Haan, D. D. (2016) 'Where Does Avicenna Demonstrate the Existence of God?', *Arabic Sciences and Philosophy*, 26(1), pp. 97–128.

Hamri, S. (2018) 'On the Ultimate Ground of Being', *International Journal for Philosophy of Religion*, 83(2), pp. 161–8.

Hamri, S. (2019) 'The Modal Symmetry First Cause Argument', *Religious Studies*, 55(1), pp. 77–84.

Hestevold, H. S. (1993) 'The Anselmian "Single-Divine-Attribute Doctrine"', *Religious Studies*, 29(1), pp. 63–77.

Hourani, G. F. (1972) 'Ibn Sīnā on Necessary and Possible Existence', *The Philosophical Forum*, 4(1), pp. 74–86.

Janos, D. (2020) *Avicenna on the Ontology of Pure Quiddity*. Berlin: De Gruyter.

Jenkins, C. S. (2011) 'Is Metaphysical Dependence Irreflexive?', *The Monist*, 94(2), pp. 267–76.

Johnson, S. A. (1984) 'Ibn Sīnā's Fourth Ontological Argument for God's Existence', *The Muslim World*, 74(3–4), pp. 161–71.

Jolivet, J. (1984) 'Aux origines de l'ontologie d'Ibn Sina', in Jolivet, J., and Rashed, R. (eds.) *Etudes sur Avicenne*. Paris: Belles Lettres, pp. 19–28.

Kamal, M. (2016) 'Avicenna's Necessary Being', *Open Journal of Philosophy*, 6, pp. 194–200.

Kaplan, D. (1979) 'On the Logic of Demonstratives', *Journal of Philosophical Logic*, 8, pp. 81–98.

Kaukua, J. (2020) 'The Flying and the Masked Man, One More Time: Comments on Peter Adamson and Fedor Benevich, "The Thought

Experimental Method: Avicenna's Flying Man Argument"', *Journal of the American Philosophical Association*, 6(3), pp. 285–96.

al-Kindī (2012) *The Philosophical Works of al-Kindī*. Translated by P. Adamson and P. E. Pormann. Karachi: Oxford University Press.

Kripke, S. A. (1980) *Naming and Necessity*. Cambridge, MA: Harvard University Press.

Legenhausen, H. M. (2005) 'The Proof of the Sincere', *Journal of Islamic Philosophy*, 1(1), pp. 44–61.

Logan, I. (2009) *Reading Anselm's Proslogion: The History of Anselm's Argument and Its Significance Today*. Aldershot: Ashgate.

Macierowski, E. M. (1988) 'Does God Have a Quiddity According to Avicenna?', *The Thomist: A Speculative Quarterly Review*, 52(1), pp. 79–87.

Mackie, J. L. (1982) *The Miracle of Theism: Arguments for and against the Existence of God*. Oxford: Clarendon.

Marmura, M. E. (1960) 'Avicenna and the Problem of the Infinite Number of Souls', *Mediaeval Studies*, 22, pp. 232–9.

Marmura, M. E. (1964) 'Avicenna's Theory of Prophecy in the Light of Ash'arite Theology', in McCullough, W. S. (ed.) *The Seed of Wisdom*. Toronto: Toronto University Press, pp. 159–78.

Marmura, M. E. (1980) 'Avicenna's Proof from Contingency for God's Existence in the Metaphysics of the Shifā''', *Mediaeval Studies*, 42, pp. 337–52.

Marmura, M. E. (1984) 'Avicenna on Primary Concepts in the Metaphysics of his al-Shifā''', in Savory, R. M. and Agius, D. A. (eds.) *Logos Islamikos*. Toronto: Pontifical Institute of Mediaeval Studies, pp. 219–39.

Marmura, M. E. (1986) 'Avicenna's "Flying Man" in Context', *The Monist*, 69 (3), pp. 383–95.

Marmura, M. E. and Rist, J. M. (1963) 'Al-Kindī's Discussion of Divine Existence and Oneness', *Mediaeval Studies*, 25, pp. 338–54.

Mayer, T. (2001) 'Ibn Sīnā's "Burhān al-Siddīqīn"', *Journal of Islamic Studies*, 12(1), pp. 18–39.

Mayer, T. (2003) 'Faḫr ad-Dīn ar-Rāzī's Critique of Ibn Sīnā's Argument for the Unity of God in the Išārāt, and Naṣīr ad-Dīn aṭ-Ṭūsī's Defence', in Reisman, D. C. and Al-Rahim, A. H. (eds.) *Before and after Avicenna: Proceedings of the First Conference of the Avicenna Study Group*. Leiden: Brill, pp. 199–218.

McGinnis, J. (2010a) *Avicenna*. Oxford: Oxford University Press.

McGinnis, J. (2010b) 'Avicennan Infinity: A Select History of the Infinite through Avicenna', *Documenti e studi sulla tradizione filosofica medieval*, 21, pp. 199–221.

McGinnis, J. (2011) 'The Ultimate Why Question: Avicenna on Why God Is Absolutely Necessary', in Wippel, J. (ed.) *The Ultimate Why Question: Why Is There Anything at All Rather Than Nothing Whatsoever?* Washington, DC: Catholic University of America Press, pp. 65–83.

Mcginnis, J., and Reisman, D. (2007) *Classical Arabic Philosophy: An Anthology of Sources.* Indianapolis, IN: Hackett.

McNabb, T. D. (2019) *Religious Epistemology.* Cambridge: Cambridge University Press.

Menn, S. (2011) 'Fārābī in the Reception of Avicenna's Metaphysics: Averroes against Avicenna on Being and Unity', in Hasse, D. N., and Bertolacci, A. (eds.) *The Arabic, Hebrew and Latin Reception of Avicenna's Metaphysics.* Berlin: De Gruyter, pp.51–96.

Morewedge, P. (1970) 'Ibn Sina Avicenna and Malcolm and the Ontological Argument', *The Monist*, 54(2), pp. 234–49.

Morewedge, P. (1980) 'A Third Version of the Ontological Argument in the Ibn Sinian Metaphysics', in Morewedge, P. (ed.) *Islamic Philosophical Theology.* New York: State University of New York Press, pp. 165–87.

Morris, T. V (1987) 'Perfect Being Theology', *Noûs*, 21(1), pp. 19–30.

Morvarid, M. (2008) 'Allamah Tabtaba'i's Siddiqin Argument of God: A Critical Look', in Kanzian, C. and Legenhausen, M. (eds.) *Proofs for the Existence of God: Contexts, Structures, Relevance.* Innsbruck: Innsbruck University Press, pp. 49–56.

Morvarid, M. (2021) 'Siddiqin Argument', in Goetz, S. and Taliaferro, C. (eds.) *The Encyclopedia of Philosophy of Religion.* New York: Wiley Blackwell.

Nagasawa, Y. (2017) *Maximal God: A New Defence of Perfect Being Theism.* Oxford: Oxford University Press.

Nasr, S. H. (ed.) (2015) *The Study Quran: A New Translation and Commentary.* San Francisco: HarperOne.

Oppy, G. (1995) *Ontological Arguments and Belief in God.* Cambridge: Cambridge University Press.

Plantinga, A. (1974) *The Nature of Necessity.* Oxford: Oxford University Press.

Plantinga, A. (1977) *God, Freedom, and Evil.* New York: Harper & Row.

Plantinga, A. (1981) 'Is Belief in God Properly Basic?', *Noûs*, 15(1), pp. 41–51.

Plantinga, A. (1983) 'Reason and Belief in God', in Plantinga, A., and Wolterstorff, N. (eds.) *Faith and Rationality.* Notre Dame: University of Notre Dame Press, pp. 16–93.

Pruss, A. R., and Rasmussen, J. L. (2018) *Necessary Existence, Necessary Existence.* Oxford: Oxford University Press.

Rashed, R. (2008) 'The Philosophy of Mathematics', in Rahman, S., Street, T., and Tahiri, H. (eds.) *The Unity of Science in the Arabic Tradition: Science, Logic, Epistemology and Their Interactions.* Dordrecht: Springer, pp. 153–82.

Rasmussen, J. L. (2018) 'Plantinga', in Oppy, G. (ed.) *Ontological Arguments*. Cambridge: Cambridge University Press, pp. 176–94.

Richardson, K. (2013) 'Avicenna's Conception of the Efficient Cause', *British Journal for the History of Philosophy A*, 21(2), pp. 220–39.

Richardson, K. (2014) 'Avicenna and the Principle of Sufficient Reason', *The Review of Metaphysics*, 67(4), pp. 743–68.

Rizvi, S. (2019) 'Mulla Sadra', *The Stanford Encyclopedia of Philosophy*. Edited by E. N. Zalta. Available at https://plato.stanford.edu/archives/spr2019/entries/mulla-sadra/.

Rogers, K. A. (2000) *Perfect Being Theology*. Edinburgh: Edinburgh University Press.

Rosen, G. (2010) 'Metaphysical Dependence: Grounding and Reduction', in Hale, B., and Hoffmann, A. (eds.) *Modality: Metaphysics, Logic, and Epistemology*. Oxford: Oxford University Press, pp. 109–35.

Rosheger, J. P. (2002) 'Is God a "What"? Avicenna, William of Auvergne, and Aquinas on the Divine Essence', in Iglis, J. (ed.) *Medieval Philosophy and the Classical Tradition in Islam, Judaism and Christianity*. London: Routledge, pp. 277–96.

Schaffer, J. (2009) 'On What Grounds What', in Chalmers, D., Manley, D., and Wasserman, R. (eds.) *Metametaphysics: New Essays on the Foundations of Ontology*. Oxford: Oxford University Press, pp. 347–83.

Schlesinger, G. N. (1988) *New Perspectives on Old-Time Religion*. Oxford: Clarendon.

Shihadeh, A. (2008) 'The Existence of God', in Winter, T. (ed.) *The Cambridge Companion to Classical Islamic Theology*. Cambridge: Cambridge University Press, pp. 197–217.

Sobel, J. H. (2004) *Logic and Theism: Arguments For and Against Beliefs in God*. Cambridge: Cambridge University Press.

Speaks, J. (2018) *The Greatest Possible Being*. Oxford: Oxford University Press.

Street, T. (2002) 'An Outline of Avicenna's Syllogistic', *Archiv für Geschichte der Philosophie*, 84(2), pp. 129–60.

Street, T. (2013) 'Avicenna on the Syllogism', in Adamson, P. (ed.) *Interpreting Avicenna: Critical Essays*. Cambridge: Cambridge University Press, pp. 48–70.

Swinburne, R. (1988) 'Could There Be More Than One God?', *Faith and Philosophy*, 5(3), pp. 225–41.

Vance, C. (2020) 'The World Is a Necessary Being', *Philosophia*, 48(1), pp. 377–90.

Waterlow, S. (1982) *Passage and Possibility: A Study of Aristotle's Modal Concepts*. Oxford: Oxford University Press.

Wierenga, E. R. (1989) *The Nature of God: An Inquiry into Divine Attribute.* Ithaca, NY: Cornell University Press.

Williamson, T. (2013) *Modal Logic As Metaphysics.* Oxford: Oxford University Press.

Wisnovsky, R. (2000) 'Notes on Avicenna's Concept of Thingness (Šayʾiyya)', *Arabic Sciences and Philosophy*, 10(2), pp. 181–221.

Wisnovsky, R. (2003) *Avicenna's Metaphysics in Context, Journal of Chemical Information and Modeling.* Ithaca, NY: Cornell University Press.

Wisnovsky, R. (2005) 'Avicenna', in Adamson, P., and Taylor, R. C. (eds.) *The Cambridge Companion to Arabic Philosophy.* Cambridge: Cambridge University Press, pp. 92–136.

Zagzebski, L. T. (2007) *The Philosophy of Religion: An Historical Introduction.* Oxford: Blackwell.

Zarepour, M. S. (2016) 'Avicenna on the Nature of Mathematical Objects', *Dialogue: Canadian Philosophical Review*, 55(3), pp. 511–36.

Zarepour, M. S. (2020a) 'Avicenna's Notion of Fiṭrīyāt: A Comment on Dimitri Gutas' Interpretation', *Philosophy East and West*, 70(3), pp. 819–33.

Zarepour, M. S. (2020b) 'Avicenna on Mathematical Infinity', *Archiv für Geschichte der Philosophie.*

Zarepour, M. S. (2020c) 'Non-innate A Priori Knowledge in Avicenna', *Philosophy East and West*, 70(3), pp. 841–8.

Zarepour, M. S. (2021) 'Infinite Magnitudes, Infinite Multitudes, and the Beginning of the Universe', *Australasian Journal of Philosophy*, 99(3), pp. 472–89.

Acknowledgements

I would like to dedicate this Element to my awesome parents, Zahra Gholamian Abahari and Ali Asghar Zarepour. In addition to them, there are many other people whom I have to thank here. I am grateful, as always, to my lifelong teacher Ali Jahankhah, for having drawn my attention to the philosophical discussions around the Islamic conception of monotheism when I was a high school student. I came to learn of Anselmian perfect being theology through my late wise friend Mahdi Bagherpour; I am indebted to him for this, as well as for much else besides. The idea of cashing out the Avicennian notion of efficient causation in terms of the notion of ontological grounding came to me during a thought-provoking after-lunch conversation with Tony Street and Asad Q. Ahmed at Clare Hall, Cambridge, and I owe them considerable thanks. In preparing the final version of the Element, I benefitted from extremely helpful comments and suggestions by Tony Street and three anonymous reviewers, to all whom I am very grateful. This Element has come into existence mainly because of the generous support of the John Templeton Foundation: I started working on it in summer 2020 after receiving a research award from the Theology, Science, and Knowledge project directed by Jon McGinnis and Billy Dunaway and funded by the John Templeton Foundation and the University of Missouri–St. Louis; the Element was completed in March 2021, a few months after I joined The Global Philosophy of Religion project as a postdoctoral researcher in Islamic philosophy of religion; this project, directed by Yujin Nagasawa at the University of Birmingham, was also funded by the John Templeton Foundation. I am greatly indebted to the John Templeton Foundation and to the directors of these projects. I would also like to thank Paul Moser and Chad Meister, the editors of the Cambridge Elements in Religion and Monotheism series. Finally, I express my deepest gratitude to my family and friends, and in particular to my wife, Samaneh, without whose unconditional support this Element would not have seen the light of day. A few days before writing these lines, the Necessary Existent gave us a baby girl, Sophia, who brought joy and hope to our world. I am thankful to her too. *Wa-l-ḥamdu li-l-lāhi awwalan wa āḫirā.*

Cambridge Elements ≡

Religion and Monotheism

Paul K. Moser

Loyola University Chicago

Paul K. Moser is Professor of Philosophy at Loyola University Chicago. He is the author of *Understanding Religious Experience; The God Relationship; The Elusive God* (winner of national book award from the Jesuit Honor Society); *The Evidence for God; The Severity of God; Knowledge and Evidence* (all Cambridge University Press); and *Philosophy after Objectivity* (Oxford University Press); co-author of *Theory of Knowledge* (Oxford University Press); editor of *Jesus and Philosophy* (Cambridge University Press) and *The Oxford Handbook of Epistemology* (Oxford University Press); co-editor of *The Wisdom of the Christian Faith* (Cambridge University Press). He is the co-editor with Chad Meister of the book series Cambridge Studies in Religion, Philosophy, and Society.

Chad Meister

Bethel University

Chad Meister is Professor of Philosophy and Theology and Department Chair at Bethel College. He is the author of *Introducing Philosophy of Religion* (Routledge, 2009), *Christian Thought: A Historical Introduction*, 2nd edition (Routledge, 2017), and *Evil: A Guide for the Perplexed*, 2nd edition (Bloomsbury, 2018). He has edited or co-edited the following: *The Oxford Handbook of Religious Diversity* (Oxford University Press, 2010), *Debating Christian Theism* (Oxford University Press, 2011), with Paul Moser, *The Cambridge Companion to the Problem of Evil* (Cambridge University Press, 2017), and with Charles Taliaferro, *The History of Evil* (Routledge 2018, in six volumes).

About the Series

This Cambridge Element series publishes original concise volumes on monotheism and its significance. Monotheism has occupied inquirers since the time of the biblical patriarchs, and it continues to attract interdisciplinary academic work today. Engaging, current, and concise, the Elements benefit teachers, researchers, and advanced students in religious studies, biblical studies, theology, philosophy of religion, and related fields.

Cambridge Elements ≡

Religion and Monotheism

A full series listing is available at: www.cambridge.org/er&m

Printed in the United States
by Baker & Taylor Publisher Services